IBCCrim Studies in Criminal Law, Human Rights and Criminology

Volume 1

The IBCCrim Studies in Criminal Law, Human Rights and Criminology seeks to leverage diverse and innovative work both within and beyond the boundaries of criminology and human rights studies, with specific attention to approaches inspired by both traditional movements and more recent movements focused on building an effective and equitable criminal justice system.

Human rights in contexts such as improved prison conditions, the implementation of restorative criminal public policies, and social transformation through a criminal law based on the protection of individuals and minorities are fundamental. These aspects play a central role in issues of equality, justice, and combating discrimination. These dimensions must be analyzed in all their linguistic, logical, and theoretical aspects.

Through the lens of human rights, the series aims to publish works that explore the intrinsic link between criminal justice and human rights, fostering perspectives that can be defined as inclusive and progressive, especially in the sense of transforming penal practice and reimagining a system that understands individual and cultural complexity, not reducing subjects to a single dominant narrative, with a focus on works that prioritize a humanized and restorative criminal law.

The main objective of the series is to build on human rights and restorative justice theories to propose a transformative perspective on criminal legal science and methodology. In pursuing these tasks, the series aims to engage with the connections between identity, social relations, and political systems, and with all the social aspects that interact in the construction and representation of difference through language and human actions.

The series welcomes proposals—whether edited collections or single-author monographs—that emphasize the conflicts and connections between justice, criminal law, and minority protection, proposing critical approaches to law and human rights studies, offering analyses in areas such as legal theory, philosophy and sociology of law, criminal law, criminal procedure, and human rights.

Louise de Barros Ibarra Papa

Prevention of Human Rights Violations in the Corporate Sphere

Perspectives on Criminal Compliance and Corporate Criminal Liability

Springer

Louise de Barros Ibarra Papa
Universidade Federal do Mato Grosso
Cuiabá, Mato Grosso, Brazil

ISSN 3059-4332 ISSN 3059-4340 (electronic)
IBCCrim Studies in Criminal Law, Human Rights and Criminology
ISBN 978-3-032-06212-3 ISBN 978-3-032-06213-0 (eBook)
https://doi.org/10.1007/978-3-032-06213-0

The original submitted manuscript has been translated into English. The translation was done using artificial intelligence. A subsequent revision was performed by the author(s) to further refine the work and to ensure that the translation is appropriate concerning content and scientific correctness. It may, however, read stylistically different from a conventional translation.

This Springer imprint is published by the registered company Springer Nature Switzerland AG.
The registered company address is: Gewerbestrasse 11, 6330 Cham, Switzerland

To my beloved grandmother "Cici", whose absence was felt throughout the writing of this

Contents

Abbreviations

ANM	National Mining Agency
BHR	Business and Human Rights
CLLE	Criminal Liability of Legal Entities
COSO	Committee of Sponsoring Organizations of the Treadway Commission
CSR	Corporate Social Responsibility
ECL	Economic Criminal Law
ENCCLA	National Strategy for Combating Corruption and Money Laundering
FATF/GAFI	Financial Action Group against Money Laundering and Terrorism Financing
GDP	Gross Domestic Product
GRECO	Group of States against Corruption
ISO	International Organization for Standardization
OECD	Organisation for Economic Co-operation and Development
PC	Penal Code
PNLD	National Programme for Training and Capacity Building to Combat Corruption and Money Laundering
SRSG	Secretary-General on the Issue of Human Rights and Transnational Corporations and Other Business Enterprises

---

Editor's note: In this publication, certain acronyms have been retained in their original form, either in Portuguese or as internationally recognized abbreviations. This editorial choice was made for two main reasons:

Institutional Reference: Some acronyms refer to official Brazilian programs, agencies, or legal concepts whose original abbreviations are widely used and identifiable within the national context (e.g., ENCCLA, PNLD).

Global Recognition: Other acronyms correspond to international organizations or frameworks whose abbreviations are standardized and commonly used across languages (e.g., OECD, ISO, FATF, GRECO).

As a result, readers may notice that the acronym does not always match the translated name of the institution or concept. This is intentional and aims to preserve clarity, consistency, and alignment with academic and institutional usage.

Chapter 1
Introduction

Where is the moral indignation over corporate crime?[1] This was the question posed by American criminologist William Laufer in his identically titled 2014 publication. With this, he sparked a reflection on the insufficient moral disapproval within the criminal justice system towards irregularities carried out by corporations and the failure of corporate criminal law in the prosecution and punishment of corporate crime. Consequently, there is a current need to focus on corporate responsibility for its socially harmful activities.

It is for this reason that this book begins with the observation of the current scenario of frequent corporate scandals, which often extend the platform of corporate criminality to serious human rights violations. Among many cases, one can cite, for example: environmental and social devastations caused in Mariana/MG and Brumadinho/MG; environmental and social impacts resulting from illegal mining (e.g., Pinheiro/Braskem Case); exploitation of workers by large clothing companies (e.g., Zara Case); lack of workplace safety (Case of the Employees of the Santo Antônio de Jesus Fireworks Factory and their families vs. Brazil); contamination of rivers and soils by toxic material (e.g., Chevron/Texaco Case in Ecuador); use of asbestos in industrial production (Asbestos Case); the leakage and improper use of user data by Big Techs (e.g., Facebook); the use of improper material in food manufacturing (e.g., Operation Weak Meat); manipulation of toxic product emissions (Volkswagen Case), etc.[2]

[1] Unless otherwise indicated, all translations of quoted material from foreign languages into English are the authors' own. These are marked throughout the text with the expression our translation following the citation. Original quotations may be provided in footnotes when relevant for clarity or interpretation.

[2] In Brazil, recent news indicates the persistence of the exploitation of workers in conditions analogous to slavery in the productive chain of coffee and wineries: https://www.business-humanrights.org/pt/%C3%BAltimas-not%C3%ADcias/brasil-trabalho-escravo-sustenta-lucros-na-cadeia-global-do-caf%C3%A9-revela-pesquisa/; https://reporterbrasil.org.br/2025/04/escravizados-vinho-justica-rs-condena-terceirizada-3-milhoes/.

L. d. B. Ibarra Papa, *Prevention of Human Rights Violations in the Corporate Sphere*, IBCCrim Studies in Criminal Law, Human Rights and Criminology 1,
https://doi.org/10.1007/978-3-032-06213-0_1

In the context of globalisation, large corporations, notably transnational and multinational, have expanded their activities in a significant and staggered circulation of goods and capital, emerging as true agents of international law, whose assets often exceed the Gross Domestic Product (GDP) of several nation-states. Such is the case with Apple, which is wealthier (US$2.2 trillion) than Italy (US $2 trillion), Brazil (US$2 trillion) and Canada (US$1.8 trillion); Microsoft (US $1.8 trillion), which surpasses the revenue of Russia (US$1.6 trillion), South Korea (US$1.6 trillion) and Australia (US$1.3 trillion); and Amazon (US$1.6 trillion), which outstrips Spain (US$1.3 trillion) and Mexico (US$1.2 trillion).[3]

One cannot ignore the economic potential of the activities carried out by large corporations, especially those that operate globally through their subsidiaries and with the decentralisation of their offices at the multinational level. However, the reflections brought forth in this paper stem from the observation that these entities, while emerging as influential actors in the international reality, open a new field of discussion about the human and environmental costs of corporate globalisation,[4] especially from the perspective of the absence of an effective regulatory framework to counter their potentially socially harmful behaviours.

Naturally, the matter has been raised and discussed on numerous fronts, both internationally and nationally (Brazil). Noteworthy is the entry into force, on 25 July 2024, of Directive (EU) 2024/1760 of the European Parliament and the Council of Europe,[5] which guides the duty of corporate diligence in its value chain in terms of human rights, with a view to 'prioritising, preventing, mitigating, ceasing, minimising and repairing the negative, real or potential, effects on human rights and the environment resulting from the operations of the companies themselves'.[6] In Brazil, Bill No. 572/2022 stands out, which aims to create the National Framework on Human Rights and Companies.[7]

Although these are significant advances in the matter and deserve detailed analysis of their valuable institutes, the focus of this paper is the lack of depth in the field of criminal responsibility and its corresponding sanctions. Although there is provision for corporate responsibility for potential damages to human rights, such imposition applies only to the civil liability regime, with provision solely for pecuniary sanctions and public declarations of responsibility, as stated in Art. 27.3 of Directive 2024/1760. In Bill 572/2022, the provisions of responsibility, set out in Art. 18, appear to be oriented solely towards the pecuniary and corporate field.

---

[3] Cohen (2021).

[4] The relevance of the theme is the subject of specific works carried out by the United Nations High Commissioner for Human Rights (OHCHR). For detailed information: https://www.ohchr.org/en/business-and-human-rights.

[5] For details of the approved text, access: https://eur-lex.europa.eu/eli/dir/2024/1760/oj.

[6] Considering (16) of Directive (EU) 2024/1760.

[7] For details of the works, access: https://www.camara.leg.br/proposicoesWeb/fichadetramitacao?idProposicao=2317904.

Thus, when carried out in the field of responsibilities, socially harmful corporate activities take on a different contour when observed through the spectrum of criminal law and the increasingly current context of these corporations' involvement in the particular sphere of corruption—broadly and generally understood as corporate criminal actions in the economic sphere, that is, actions that involve a whole series of offences and irregularities beyond active and passive corruption crimes, for example, influence peddling, bribery, embezzlement, abuse of function or position, use of privileged information, falsification of financial information, irregularities in the securities market, illicit enrichment, subsidising irregularities, etc.[8]

Theoretical efforts have been dedicated to combining, in a multidisciplinary analysis, the close relationship between corruption, human rights and companies; that is, to examine to what extent corporate activity is involved not only in corporate crime but also in human rights violations, so as to implicate it in a new panorama of responsibilities.

Thus, this book aims not only to understand the relationship between companies and human rights but also seeks to provide insights on corporate corruption, notably to understand to what extent the penal system addresses corporate delinquency, in order to verify if it is possible to make joint efforts in the prevention of legal-penal goods and human rights.

The integration of the parameters 'company', 'corruption' and 'human rights' aims to instruct, in a more effective and coercive way, corporations to treat their self-regulatory prevention mechanisms as fertile ground for safeguarding against corporate crimes and also as components for the precaution of human rights, so as to elevate their activity beyond the purely private and economic scope and to make them assume their role as true social agents on a new civilisational, moral and ethical level.

It is under this scenario that the problematisation of the present research emerges: What are the influences of criminal sciences in the context of human rights violations by companies? Can criminal compliance be a tool for preventing corporate crimes and human rights violations? Would the criminal liability of the legal entity contribute to improving the effectiveness of compliance programmes?

The positive affirmation of the questions posed highlights the initial hypotheses of this research. These hypotheses will, for the most part, be analysed from the perspectives of criminal sciences, notably economic criminal law in the compliance era, economic criminology and corporate victimology.

Thus, the aim is to build bridges that allow for understanding corruption in relation to corporate or economic crimes, adopting perspectives of criminal policy, dogmatics and corporate criminology as a way to assimilate the criminal phenomenon within corporate frameworks, especially as a means to establish the fundamental aegis that will contribute to the critical analysis of compliance programmes and the criminal liability of the legal entity.

---

[8] This delimitation follows the line of Claudia Barrilari. Barrilari (2018).

The methodological difficulty in establishing points of convergence to the objects of analysis is not forgotten, especially when each one has a wide field of theoretical depth, requiring more precise and deep incursions. These, therefore, perhaps require greater systematic acuity, incompatible, at the moment, with the limits of the present work.

However, given the limitations of the research, the work was established around three major arcs: (i) the analysis of the relationship between the protection of human rights and corporate activity (or more simply, 'companies and human rights'); (ii) the analysis of the relationship between corporations and the practice of acts of corruption and corporate crimes (or simply 'companies and corruption'); and (iii) the analysis of the relationship between corporations and compliance instruments, and their connection with the criminal liability of the legal entity (briefly 'companies and prevention').

The arc 'Companies and Human Rights' is fundamentally set out in Chap. 2, which assumes human rights as a topic of global importance to international society. Thus, it proposes the analysis of the current scenario of defence of these rights, which, in the face of the crisis of national states and the fragility of their internal systems, is demanding new paths of protection, especially in the face of the emergence of the new global actor: corporations.

Thus, still in Chap. 2, it discusses the relationship between business activity and the violation of human rights, as well as international regulatory attempts to combine efforts to hold companies accountable for potential damages caused, and the fundamental role of corporate prevention.

Chapter 3 is guided by the overarching theme 'companies and corruption,' aiming initially to establish an intersection between 'corporations, human rights and corruption' to understand the influences of international law in the fight against corruption.

These are pertinent inferences to, in a second moment, assimilate corruption from corporate illegality, with incursions about (i) criminal policy in relation to current economic criminal law, (ii) economic criminology as a source of theories of corporate crime and (iii) corporate victimology as a possible guiding vector for compliance programmes aimed at the effective prevention of human rights violations.

From these ideas, it is proposed in Chap. 4 to analyse the arc 'companies and prevention' in order to understand the phenomenon of corporate self-regulation and the instrumentalisation of compliance programmes, as well as to infer the need for the formulation of effective prevention and restoration mechanisms, and to what extent criminal sciences can contribute to such a goal.

The work concludes with a brief analysis regarding the liability of companies in relation to *corporate crimes*, aiming to stimulate corporate self-regulation through the adoption of *compliance* mechanisms. In this way, the models of criminal liability of the legal person are presented, and the autonomous liability of the legal person is adopted as a possible *law enforcement* measure for the adoption of more effective compliance programmes, either for the prevention of economic crimes or for the prevention of human rights violations.

Finally, it is important to make specific observations about conceptual aspects, textual aspects and methodological cuts of the work.

It is noted that the research was carried out in Brazil, so that, for the most part, the Brazilian legal panorama is taken into consideration. However, it does not abstain from pointing out international theoretical influences, with mentions of other systems and legal regulations.

In conceptual terms, it is assumed, from the outset, that when mentioning 'corruption', it is referring to a broad and multifactorial phenomenon, with a clear approach to economic crimes in general. Also, when it says 'corporations' or 'companies', it is referring to medium and large-scale economic activities, with great socially harmful potential, especially those whose legal nature is affiliated with 'limited company' (Ltd) and 'public limited company' (PLC).

In textual terms, it was chosen to adopt referential notes, which, for this work, assume a character of utmost relevance, not only as a reference to the bibliographic material, but also, and substantially, as a complement to the main text (explanatory note), to assist the reader in a more vertical understanding of the theoretical contributions adopted. For this reason, future readers are advised, from the outset, to assume the explanatory notes as fundamental elements for a complete understanding of the writing.

Regarding the methodological cuts, it is noted that, given the breadth of the theme and the multidisciplinary incursions involved, it was necessary, inevitably, to distance certain theoretical contributions, although they are fundamental to a universal analysis of the theme; the limits of the work required it.

References

Books & Theses

Barrilari, C. (2018). *Crime empresarial, autorregulação e compliance*. Thomson Reuters

Journal Articles

Cohen, J. (2021). World's most valuable tech companies are richer than most countries. *PCMagazine*. https://www.pcmag.com/news/worlds-most-valuable-tech-companies-are-richer-than-most-countries

Legal Documents

European Union. (2024). Directive (EU) 2024/1760. *Official Journal of the European Union*. https://eur-lex.europa.eu/eli/dir/2024/1760/oj

Online Sources

Business & Human Rights Resource Centre. (2025). Brazil: Slave labor sustains profits in global coffee chain, research reveals. https://www.business-humanrights.org/pt/%C3%BAltimas-not%C3%ADcias/brasil-trabalho-escravo-sustenta-lucros-na-cadeia-global-do-caf%C3%A9-revela-pesquisa/

Chamber of Deputies of Brazil. (2025). Legislative proposal details. https://www.camara.leg.br/proposicoesWeb/fichadetramitacao?idProposicao=2317904

OHCHR. (2025). *Business and human rights*. United Nations High Commissioner for Human Rights. https://www.ohchr.org/en/business-and-human-rights

Repórter Brasil (2025). Enslaved in wineries: RS court orders outsourced company to pay R $3 million. https://reporterbrasil.org.br/2025/04/escravizados-vinho-justica-rs-condena-terceirizada-3-milhoes/

Chapter 2
Corporations and Human Rights

Before we reach the crux of the relationship between corporations, business crimes and human rights, it is essential that we briefly address some questions about the protection of human rights in the context of globalisation, given the current domestic and international legal landscape. This will allow us to bring forth some critical reflections on the topic.

2.1 Human Rights as a Global Issue

Human rights, as a paradigm and ethical reference guiding the international order,[1] have reached the level of legitimate international interest following two major revolutionary milestones, referred to as 'revolutions in the process of internationalising human rights': the first after the end of the Second World War and the second with the end of the Cold War.[2]

It is clear that the affirmation and consolidation of human rights as a global issue[3] and a matter of international concern requires not only their universalisation or internationalisation, but also the implementation of these rights, that is, the formulation of an international system of monitoring and control, known as *international accountability*.[4]

[1] Piovesan and Gonzaga (2019).

[2] Piovesan (2016).

[3] For more details, including political aspects: Alves (1994). Among other advancements, the author points to the substantial importance given by the Vienna Conference (and Declaration) on Human Rights of 1993 to the 'recognition of the legitimacy of international concern with the promotion and protection of human rights'(our translation).

[4] Piovesan (2016), p. 251.

L. d. B. Ibarra Papa, *Prevention of Human Rights Violations in the Corporate Sphere*,
IBCCrim Studies in Criminal Law, Human Rights and Criminology 1,
https://doi.org/10.1007/978-3-032-06213-0_2

The normative structure of protection was thus sought from the UN Charter of 1945, which, in its Article 55, clause 'c', established that the United Nations (Member States) would promote 'universal respect for, and observance of, human rights and fundamental freedoms for all'.[5] However, the issue was only effectively inaugurated by the landmark Universal Declaration of Human Rights of 1948, which set out the rights and fundamental freedoms to be guaranteed.

At the time, the need to implement legally binding obligations to the provisions of the 1948 Declaration was discussed, much like an international treaty. Thus, in 1966, the drafting of two international treaties (the International Covenant on Civil and Political Rights and the International Covenant on Economic, Social and Cultural Rights) was completed, which incorporated legally binding and obligatory provisions for the rights set out in the Declaration. The combination of these instruments was called the International Bill of Rights and inaugurated the global system of protection for these rights—which is still being expanded today through the formulation of multiple special-scope treaties and non-conventional global protection mechanisms (such as Resolutions).[6]

This global system is complemented by regional protection systems, which internationalise human rights in a geographically specific way at the regional level in Europe, America and Africa. Each has its own legal apparatus and bodies, which contribute to the construction of a multi-level protection system[7] through complementary and coordinated action between them and the global and national protection systems.[8]

Under this instrumental universe of protection, the contemporary conception of human rights is formulated,[9] which seeks a new paradigm of cooperation between countries with the aim of enforcing the basic rights of every human being and achieving a global level of safeguarding their dignity—celebrating a 'culture of rights' based on the observance of an 'irreducible ethical minimum'[10] and achieving a 'confluence universalism'.[11]

---

[5] Brazil (1945) Decree No. 19,841, of 22 October 1945. Promulgates the United Nations Charter. Presidency of the Republic, Brasília. http://www.planalto.gov.br/ccivil_03/decreto/1930-1949/d19841.htm. Accessed April 2025.

[6] Piovesan (2016), pp. 251–254, 282, 336.

[7] Piovesan (2016), p. 394.

[8] Mazzuoli (2018) *Curso de direitos humanos*, 5th rev, updated and expanded edn. Método Publisher, São Paulo, pp. 68–69.

[9] For a more detailed understanding of this concept, see: Piovesan and Gonzaga (2019), p. 63.

[10] Piovesan (2016), p. 394.

[11] Term coined by Joaquín Herrera Flores when critically analysing the contemporary conception of human rights. The author points to the need to overcome the 'controversy between the alleged universalism of rights and the apparent particularity of cultures', since both conceptions are 'products of reductionist visions of reality'. Thus, he proposes a rationality of resistance in which there is not a 'universalism of departure' or a 'universalism of parallel lines', but rather an intercultural dialogue. 'A rationality that does not deny that it is possible to arrive at a universal synthesis of the different options relating to rights. And it does not discard the potentiality of struggles for the recognition of ethnic or gender differences. What we deny is to consider the

The internationalisation of human rights required (and continues to require), therefore, the creation of minimum protection standards to be effectively adopted equitably by states, regardless of their internal normativity, since, being a matter of legitimate international interest, it transcends strictly domestic parameters and even calls into question the very sovereignty of states.[12]

Besides, the very concept of internationalisation already announces a certain decline in absolute state sovereignty. It is known that many of the problems faced in contemporary times have ceased to be attributed to a single State. Instead, global issues are arising that need to be resolved beyond the limits of internal sovereignty and, for some, beyond the confines of 'provincial constitutionalism'[13] or traditional law.

2.1.1 *Crisis of the State and Its Sovereignty, and the Modulation in Law for the Protection of Human Rights*

It is in the pursuit of new contours for law that Luigi Ferrajoli[14] advocates for the urgent and unavoidable construction of a global or worldwide constitutionalism as an axiological horizon for jurists, as a way of planning future guarantees, especially to remedy human rights violations. Similarly, Piovesan[15] points to the emergence of a new public law—born from the convergence of constitutional law and international public law—which promotes state openness, jurisdictional dialogue and the prevalence of human dignity in a multi-level system.

This is fundamental when observing not only the crisis of the states but also the crisis of law, because, while the dilution of borders currently exhausts national sovereignties, Law is weakened by the alteration of the system of sources, since the greater need for global integration ends up giving rise to a constitutional weakness when dealing with contemporary problems.[16] '[. . .] The State is already too large for small things and too small for large things'[17] to the point of being essential to adopt a perspective that reconciles the sovereignties in crisis and the incessant need for protection of human rights on a global scale.

Moreover, the idea of sovereignties in crisis stems from the decline of the classic concept of sovereignty itself because, if before it was possible to understand

---

universal as a starting point or a field of disagreements. The universal must be reached—universalism of arrival or of convergence—after (not before) a conflictive, discursive dialogue process [. . .]'. (our translation). Flores (2002).

[12] Mazzuoli (2018), p. 530.

[13] Neves (2014), p. 226.

[14] Ferrajoli (2002), p. 63.

[15] Piovesan (2016), p. 396.

[16] Ferrajoli (2014), p. 16.

[17] Ferrajoli (2002), p. 50.

that modern States, as so-called absolute entities, asserted their independence before international society, today, with the globalised environment[18] and with new democratic assumptions,[19] the conception of sovereignty is, at least, flexible, understood in the 'international cooperation of States for common purposes'.[20]

One cannot exclude from the analysis the fact that the crisis of modern States is also linked to the 'void of public law' faced by it due to the inversion of the relationship between public and private,[21] with the replacement of the political and democratic government of the economy by the economic government of politics. That is, by the 'total impotence of politics and [. . .] its subordination to the economy, to the so-called "markets," that is, to the deregulated powers of speculative financial capital', which 'impose on them the destruction of the *Welfare*, the reduction of the public sphere, the dismantling of labour law, the growth of inequalities and poverty and the devastation of common goods'.[22]

This scenario of 'void' and weaknesses is, without a doubt, linked to the consequences arising from economic globalisation, notably the disintegrating impact of the transnationalisation of markets on the political-institutional structures of state orders, still rooted in the aspects of sovereignty and territoriality.[23]

In the face of the polycentrism that now characterises the globalised economy, positive law—notably domestic law—loses its power of influence over the new universe of the globalised, computerised, borderless world and complex actions, because 'its standardising norms [. . .] cannot logically account for the increasingly differentiated social, economic, political and cultural situations'.[24]

---

[18] '*Globalisation* is an open and multifaceted concept, which involves problems and processes related to trade liberalisation and opening, the functional integration of internationally dispersed economic activities, interstate competition for volatile capital, and the advent of an international financial system over which governments have decreasing control'. Faria (2010), p. 1.

[19] 'The globalisation of the economy has generated interdependent relationships, in which States have been, at the very least, obliged to gather in groups, trade borders disappear and the national currency will gradually be replaced by another common instrument of exchange and buying and selling'. (our translation). Cruz (2007), p. 109.

[20] Mazzuoli (2018), p. 530.

[21] 'Thus, the relationship between public and private has been reversed: no longer the governance of private powers by public powers, but the governance of public powers by private powers. And thus, the relationship between politics and economy has been reversed. It is no longer the States, with their policies, that discipline the markets, imposing their rules, limits and ties, but the markets that discipline and govern the States. It is no longer democratically elected governments and parliaments that regulate economic life in the interest of the general public, but the markets that impose anti-democratic and anti-social policies on States, to the advantage of private interests in maximising profits, financial speculations and the plundering of common and vital goods'. (our translation) Ferrajoli (2013).

[22] Ferrajoli (2013), 1(2).

[23] '[B]y generating new forms of power, autonomous, deterritorialised, the transnationalisation of markets weakened the essential character of sovereignty [. . .] and challenged both the centrality and the exclusivity of the legal-political structures of the nation-state'. (our translation) Ferrajoli (2013), pp. 387–388.

[24] Ferrajoli (2013), p. 45.

For Ferrajoli,[25] this effect of the crisis of the old national states—almost a 'pre-modern regression to the *Patrimonial State*', determined by the collapse of the relationship between economic powers and political governing powers, no longer the former 'subordinated and regulated by the latter, but vice versa'—is a consequence of the 'lack of public rules, limits and bonds aimed at guaranteeing human rights in confrontations with the new transnational powers that have overthrown the old state powers or have subtracted them from their role of government and control'.[26]

It is evident, therefore, that the insufficiency of states in accommodating the demands of globalisation ends up compromising not only the fundamental principles of the notion of sovereignty but also its own normative system, as it progressively loses 'control of the systemic rationality of its codes by replacing traditional abstract, generic and impersonal norms with particularising, specific and finalistic norms'.[27] characteristic of the multiplication of sources of law arising from the international field. In other words, 'norms of foreign origin come to integrate the law, with their own characteristics, with the possibility of influencing national legislations, which, in this way, tend to be more flexible'.[28]

In light of this, it is important to reflect that changes in the perspectives of states and their sovereignties, under the influence of the transnational order, invariably lead to a crisis of traditional law, which, by losing its classic attributes of systematicity, generality and stability,[29] is invited to break with its modern conception in order to encompass the emergence of soluble, liquid law.[30] This new law, or the law of post-modernity, represented not by the pyramidal paradigm but by a network model, tends to convert 'into the random product of a set of interaction systems'.[31]

The law of post-modernity is, therefore, based on an integration model that, by supporting new values such as creativity, flexibility, pluralism and reciprocal learning,[32] opens up the possibility of encompassing new forms or modes of societal regulation, such as the protection of fundamental rights at the international level and also the case of corporate self-regulation (*v. infra*).

The international protection of rights is a clear reflection of the crisis of nation-states (and their sovereignties) and also of the crisis of traditional law, which no longer contains mechanisms capable of dealing with the issue sufficiently,

[25] Ferrajoli (2013), p. 387–388.

[26] Ferrajoli (2013), p. 391.

[27] Faria (1997), p. 47.

[28] Barrilari (2018), p. 190.

[29] Chevallier (2011), p. 241.

[30] Chevallier (2011), p. 247.

[31] Chevallier (2011), pp. 247–248.

[32] Chevallier cites as an example the European law that 'is thus constructed, following a flexible and pluralistic method, at the antipodes of modern unitarism', having as its north the ethical primacy of human rights. Chevallier (2011), p. 248.

composing the framework of the rise of new public law that is apt for the prevalence of dialogue and cooperation.

Undoubtedly, the consecration of international protection instruments—such as the Universal Declaration of 1948, the International Covenants of 1966 and all other human rights treaties arising from the global convention of states—was and is a milestone of international integration in favour of cooperation. This occurs not only because the decision-making capacity of the state organisation began to take into account the reaction of the transnational community, but also due to the assumption of obligations and submission by states to the control of international organisations, which, by becoming holders of competences, gradually 'empty' sovereign state power.[33]

However, critical views are needed on this new legal emergence of protection, since the promotion of a true legal and institutional integration at the international level, commensurate with the new global economic powers, must be attentive to its 'void of guarantees'. This scenario, therefore, requires 'operational norms capable of filling its gaps', as well as the development of a supranational economic policy capable of imposing rules, limits and controls on financial mechanisms.[34]

Ferrajoli[35] proposes that it is necessary, paraphrasing Ronald Dworkin, to take international law seriously, not only by assuming its principles as binding but also, and above all, by planning the institutional forms,[36] the legal guarantees, and the political strategies necessary to realise them. Thus, it is possible to truly assume the fundamental rights of man as inalienable paradigms to put an end to the great *apartheid* that excludes most of humanity from their enjoyment.[37]

For international instruments to gain greater adherence and effectiveness, surpassing the tone of 'mere rhetorical declarations', Ferrajoli conceives the idea of a common system of guarantees, which shifts the field of voluntariness of public international law to a scenario of greater enforceability as a way, even, to give rise to a planetary constitutionalism and a 'Constitution of the Earth' 'that provides guarantees and institutions commensurate with global challenges and the protection of everyone's life'.[38] For example, a virus that knows no borders is, without a shadow of a doubt, a global emergency, which depicts, at the same time, the

---

[33] Cruz (2007), p. 111.

[34] Ferrajoli (2013), p. 391–392.

[35] Ferrajoli (2002), p. 46.

[36] The author proposes a reformulation of the separation of powers, with the reinforcement and introduction of guarantee functions and institutions, with powers necessary for the exercise of the guarantee of fundamental rights stipulated in international charters. See more in: Ferrajoli (2013). p. 395.

[37] Ferrajoli (2014), p. 31.

[38] The author mentions the inauguration, in Rome, of the school 'Earth Constitution', which proposes to reaffirm the emergence of a planetary public sphere capable of dealing with current challenges, such as the Coronavirus. Ferrajoli (2020). The virus puts globalisation on its feet. *Il Manifesto*. 17 March. Available at: https://ilmanifesto.it/il-virus-mette-la-globalizzazione-con-i-piedi-per-terra/ (Original Italian version). Accessed 3 September 2021.

fragility and total interdependence of world society, questioning the need for the adoption of homogeneous solutions around the entire globe.[39]

From another perspective, the safeguarding of human rights in contemporary times requires, in addition to the re-evaluation of the role of the public international sphere, the reshuffling of the domestic law of States, which, when driven by 'top-down' processes of instruments, bodies and international courts, are obliged to re-examine their constitutional orders with a view to facing new challenges, especially as a way of converging their protection structures.[40]

'The State is not alone', as J. J. Canotilho has already announced.[41] The law—notably the constitutional law—of the post-modern State transcends its borders and enters into various other legal orders, communicating with them. In this way, at the current stage, it is essential to understand the 'new spirit of constitutionalism', which, according to the author, is called interconstitutionalism.[42] Under the aegis of this thought, 'the constitutions of the States will not disappear, but will undergo changes when inserted in the context of the interconstitutional network. This is because the State must "obey" international norms, but without losing its memory and political identity'.[43]

In this idea of approximation of legal systems, the concept of 'Cooperative Constitutional State' by Peter Härbele, as a 'necessary form of legitimate stability of tomorrow', aims to meet the needs for cooperation (economic, social and humanitarian), responsibility and international solidarity of contemporary society, in a way 'to fulfil, flexibly, its current and future tasks',[44] especially the cooperative realisation of human rights.[45] In the author's view, Constitutional Law does not begin where International Law ends, or vice versa, but rather, the Constitutional State and International Law transform together, forming a 'Common Law of Cooperation',[46] in which the 'open society'[47] should also be an internationally open society.[48]

Although Härbele, at the time, envisaged Cooperative Law from the supranational perspective of Europe, the meanings of his ideas lead us to reflect on the current need for national, regional and international orders to influence each other, so that the parts of International Law and internal Constitutional Law grow

---

[39] Ferrajoli (17 March 2020).

[40] Tushnet (2009), p. 985–1006, pp. 986–989.

[41] Canotilho (2008).

[42] The theory of interconstitutionality 'studies the interconstitutional relations of competition, convergence, juxtaposition and conflicts of various constitutions and various constituent powers in the same political space'. (Our translation). Canotilho (2008), p. 266.

[43] Ribeiro and Romancini (2015), p. 160–175, p. 164.

[44] Häberle (2007), pp. 4–5.

[45] Häberle (2007), pp. 65–70.

[46] Häberle (2007), p. 12.

[47] Häberle (1997).

[48] Häberle (2007), p. 19.

together as a whole.[49] This means that both 'the legal structures and ideas of justice of the various States of the international legal community influence the process of formation of International Law' and the 'principles and rules of International Law set, in turn, measures for the internal legal development of the State'.[50]

The fact is that both traditional Constitutional Law and classic International Law will have to handle new horizons 'to try to find an intermediate law, that better fits with the current global problems',[51] fundamentally those related to human rights. Therefore, we envisage the combination of the process of constitutionalisation of International Law and the process of internationalisation of Constitutional Law.[52]

In this context, the essentiality of developing mechanisms that enable constructive learning and mutual influence between the various legal orders of modern 'multicentric' or 'polycontextural' society is discussed,[53] fostering a cross-cutting relationship around common problems.[54]

Transconstitutionalism[55] thus proposes the interweaving between legal orders[56] without any hierarchical relationship between them.[57] In this way, through a 'conversation' or 'dialogue' across judges, courts and other powers,[58] the legal

---

[49] Häberle (2007), p. 12.

[50] Häberle (2007), p. 62.

[51] Ribeiro and Romancini (2015), p. 161.

[52] Piovesan (2013), p. 391.

[53] For transconstitutionalism, both society has a plurality of self-descriptions as the legal system itself finds various centres of self-foundation, depending on the legal order it takes as a starting point. Neves (2009), pp. 22, 35, 122.

[54] '[...] the proliferation of legal orders and the emergence of relevant trans-territorial legal cases for various legal orders: the attention these give, simultaneously, to environmental damage, to violations of human or fundamental rights, to effects of international trade and finance, to transnational crime, among other issues, makes the emergence of common cases a daily problem that affects the very reflective level and the identity of the orders involved'. (Our translation). Neves (2009), p. 128.

[55] 'State, international, supranational, transnational and local orders, considered as specific types, are unable to offer, individually, complexly adequate responses to the normative problems of world society. [...] Transconstitutionalism, as a model of intertwining that serves the transversal rationality between different legal orders, opens up to a plurality of perspectives for the solution of constitutional problems, better adapting to the relations between legal orders of the hierarchical legal system of world society'. (Our translation). Neves (2009), p. 131.

[56] The relations between public international law and state law, between supranational law and state law, between state legal orders, between state legal orders and transnational legal orders, between state legal orders and extrastate local orders and between supranational law and international law are taken into account.

[57] The orders '[...] interrelate on the reflective plane of their normative structures which are binding and have primacy', so that there is no 'downfall' or destructive/blocking action of one in relation to another. Thus, the 'mutual incorporation of contents implies a reinterpretation of meaning in the light of the receiving order'. Neves (2009), pp. 118–119.

[58] Neves mentions that, although judges and courts have leadership roles, other Powers must also participate in transconstitutionalism: '*Although the judges and courts assume a key and leading role in transconstitutional relations, these also involve the legislator, the executive power and*

systems relate in a creative exchange of solutions to common constitutional-legal problems.[59] Thus, it is certain that, when dealing with human rights, it is indispensable to adopt a multidimensional approach, elevated by the alterity between legal orders—that is, by the constant and permanent search to rearticulate their 'constitutional identities' from the perspective of the other.[60]

Beyond its theoretical contributions,[61] transconstitutional law leads us to reflect on the inevitable multiangular interweavings existing in the 'global legal system of multiple levels', especially those that involve human rights. This leads us to conclude that, nowadays, it is no longer possible to envisage the protection of these rights without taking into consideration the multiple global experiences and their legal insertions within state domestic law, especially from the interpretation of cooperative and internationally open jurisdiction.

However, it should be noted that cooperative relations between legal orders are not yet an achieved and finished goal; it is, on the contrary, a 'path' to be pursued,[62] having only occurred, so far, in some parts of the multicentric world system.[63] Thus, the limits and possibilities of the cross-cutting and cooperative relationship between the legal orders should be considered, especially in the face of possible 'overlaps' or 'oppressions' of legal orders by social systems that instrumentalise the law and, also, by the existence of asymmetries between the forms of law.[64]

There are multiple examples of these findings, but, for the purpose of this work, it is important to mention the negative dimension in the promotion of cross-cutting relations arising from the connection between law and economy/market, particularly through the (mis)management of private regimes in the forms of law, which are corrupted in favour of large multinational companies, in such a way that 'transnational legal orders [. . .] develop a type of instrumental rationality in the

---

civil society actors as well as, in some settings, members of tribal communities'. (Our translation). Neves (2017), pp. 293.

[59] Neves (2009), p. 129.

[60] Neves (2009), p. 298.

[61] Neves highlights the need for the development of a theory and a dogmatics of transconstitutional law: 'Dogmatic analyses and theoretical ventures remain very fragmented and occasional. On the methodological level, the situation remains embryonic. There are still elements of a comprehensive theory of transconstitutionalism and a comprehensive dogmatic that serves the stabilisation of transconstitutional law'. (Our translation). Neves (2009), p. 132.

[62] Häberle (2007), p. 70.

[63] '*Stable transconstitutional entanglements among legal orders have so far occurred only in a very limited portions of the "multicentric" world system in territorial of functional terms. The outlook remains unfavourable to positive developments. Nothing could be more illusory than the idea that experiences of transversal rationality in transconstitutionalism among legal orders* are *generalised or in a position to become so in the short or medium term. These experiences are part of the privileges of some legal spheres in an acutely asymmetrical world society*'. (Our translation). Neves (2017), pp. 297–298.

[64] Neves (2009), p. 279.

legal sphere' to the point of disregarding the normative claims emerging from the forms of law.[65]

In addition, Neves highlights the asymmetries in the very forms of law that involve law and economy, pointing to 'strong' market forms to the detriment of the 'weak' forms pertaining to human rights, which end up being left on the secondary legal plane both by the economy and by state protection policies, remaining as symbolic forms in world society.[66]

The fragility of the legal forms of human rights in the face of others can be associated, even, with the asymmetric relations between law and power, since there can be the 'submission' or 'subordination' of the law to the political power of the great world powers, and it can be talked about as the exploitation of legal discourses (*exploitation of legal discourses)*.[67] The consequence of this is the difficulty in normative concretisation and factual realisation of human rights, with a hypertrophy of their symbolic character to the detriment of their normative force—there is, so to speak, an insufficiency of normative force of human rights, both at the constitutional and international levels.[68]

In any case, beyond specific criticisms,[69] what is open to reflection in this topic is the fact that contemporary protection of human rights demands the formulation of a legal field that is transversal and capable of combining global integration (political, social and economic), the growing political and economic power of private sectors and the weakening of state control power. In this sense, Piovesan[70] points to the 'protection of economic, social, cultural and environmental rights versus dilemmas of economic globalisation' as one of the contemporary challenges to be faced.

---

[65] Neves (2009), p. 283.

[66] '[. . .] in the context of new developments in global society, the forms of economic law, functionally determined, are increasingly stronger than the forms of political law of the constitutional state, territorially conditioned. However, environmental law and social law, aimed at inclusion, constitute secondary forms of global society law in relation to both legal forms related to the economy and those concerning state politics'. (Our translation). Neves (2009), p. 285.

[67] Neves (2017), p. 298.

[68] From Neves' perspective, human rights *are normative expectations of generalised legal inclusion under the conditions of structural dissent in modern society.* Their symbolic strength, however, has an ambivalent character: if on the one hand it serves the normative-legal force and the realisation of human rights, on the other it contributes to prevent and hinder their legal concretisation, as well as their proper implementation. Neves (2005), 4:1–35, p. 16.

[69] 'At the moment when the categorical imperatives of market transnationalisation and democratic fullness clash and exclude each other, human rights, for this very reason, are experiencing a situation of curious ambiguity. If on the strictly legal-positive plane the panorama seems gloomy and grey, since they are being victimised by the already mentioned processes of deregulation, delegalisation and deconstitutionalisation currently promoted by nation-states to better adapt to the demands of economic globalisation, the same does not occur on the political plane. Here human rights will surely continue to constitute an important criterion to animate and guide the struggles for the revitalisation of freedom and human dignity'. (Our translation). Faria (1997), p. 52.

[70] Piovesan (2018), 1–14, p. 1.

Therefore, based on the formulation of a cooperative law that allows dialogue between various legal orders and encourages the exchange of experiences between them, the legal path(s) for the protection of human rights will be discussed in the following subsection.

2.1.2 The Path(s) for the Protection of Human Rights: The Experiences of Flexible Law and Soft Law

Although the scenario may present difficulties, it is clear that the path to be pursued is that of dialogic construction between systems or orders, especially because 'both the global system and the regional protection systems have a primary characteristic among them [. . .] which is the ability to extract values and reconcile ideas coming from different sources of production, with the aim of bringing them together in favour of safeguarding the human person'.[71]

This means that it is necessary to look at the inevitable 'modulation' of law in the face of current exchange needs—not only legal, but also from other social spheres—as a way to ensure, notably, the exchange of experiences in dealing with violations of rights and their necessary multi-level protection. Thus emerges the indispensability of a new Public Law;[72] one could speak of a new Law of Human Rights[73] or International Law of Human Rights.

Piovesan points to the crisis of traditional legal culture[74] and the emergence of a new legal paradigm, guided by the overcoming of the pyramidal legal system with the formulation of a trapezoidal legal system, in which both the Constitution and international human rights treaties are at the apex of the legal order. Furthermore, the new paradigm promotes the increasing openness of Law, with permeabilities arising from dialogue between jurisdictions, constitutional

[71] Mazzuoli (2018), p. 69.

[72] Piovesan (2016), p. 396.

[73] 'This new law imposes, in my view, irreversibly, by the combination of two significant factors: on the one hand, the express assignment of functions, by the human rights treaties themselves, to the public bodies of the State; and, on the other hand, the express reference, by an increasing number of contemporary Constitutions, to the rights enshrined in human rights treaties, incorporating them into the list of rights guaranteed at the domestic law level. Thus, international law and public law reveal an encouraging identity of purpose for the protection of the human being, and contribute to the crystallisation of the new Law of Human Rights'. (Our translation). Cançado Trindade (2016), p. 71.

[74] The author points out that the traditional paradigm is based on three essential characteristics: (a) in the pyramid with the Constitution at the apex of the legal order, in the assertion of an endogenous and self-referential legal system; (b) in the hermeticism of a purified Law, with emphasis on the internal angle of the legal order and in the strictly normative dimension; and (c) in the *state approach* (*state centered perspective*), with the valorisation of the concepts of sovereignty. Piovesan (2013), pp. 388–409, p. 390.

borrowings and interdisciplinarity, which fosters 'dialogue of Law with other knowledge and various social actors'.[75]

The new paradigm alluded to by Piovesan fits into the context of the issue of state sovereignties in crisis by proposing the overcoming of the *state approach,* with the prevalence of the *human rights approach (human-centred approach)*, that is, by the culture (and interpretation) of law guided by the expansive force of the principle of human dignity and human rights.

Under these perspectives, one of the paths for the protection of human rights is established in the dialogic construction between jurisdictions, that is, through the reciprocal exchange of experiences, especially from mutual permeabilities and jurisdictional dialogues in human rights between international and regional courts, regional and regional, regional and national, international and national and national and national.[76] Often, these dialogues arise from the three-dimensional relationship of supranational integrations, as is the case with Europe and Central America.[77]

In any case, the new legal culture should be guided by the proper exercise of conventionality control,[78] by stimulating dialogue between regional systems and horizontal dialogue between constitutional jurisdictions, not to mention the promotion of education about human rights protection systems to all agents of the State Powers (Legislative, Executive and Judicial).[79]

In this scenario of redefining the legal phenomenon, under the inspiration of the *human rights approach* and the necessary multi-level guardianship of human rights, it is more than appropriate to consider—especially for the purposes of this work—the experiences derived from supranational *soft law* norms and self-regulation instruments, as they also contribute to the formulation of a new law capable of protecting human rights in contemporary times.

[75] 'It is from the dialogue involving various knowledge and various actors that the democratisation of constitutional interpretation is verified to redefine the Law'. (Our translation). Piovesan (2013), p. 391–392.

[76] For more details: Alcalá (2013) El uso de las comunicaciones transjudiciales por parte de las jurisdicciones constitucionales em el derecho comparado y chileno. In: Bogdandy A von, Antoniazzi M, Piovesan, F (2013), p. 265; Góngora-Mera (2013) In: Bogdandy A von, Antoniazzi M, Piovesan, F (eds), p. 312; Ortega (2013). In: Bogdandy A von, Antoniazzi M, Piovesan, F (2013), p. 112.

[77] 'Therefore, when the theme of human rights protection is related to a process of regional integration within which also operates a regional convention for the protection of human rights, if there is the necessary "dialogue" between supranational courts regarding the constitutional experience of the States-parties of the integrative process, there, then, there may exist the three-dimensionality of regional integrations in their "determining elements," that is, with the irrenounceable characteristics for the subsistence of this phenomenon'. (Our translation). Carducci and Mazzuoli (2014), p. 27.

[78] For details of conventionality control: Mazzuoli (2013).

[79] Piovesan (2013), pp. 405–409.

2.2 Corporations and Human Rights

Assuming an unavoidable path of transversal dialogues, permeabilities and mutual and reciprocal exchanges, we proceed to analyse this protective architecture of human rights in the face of overcoming the classic delimitation of international protagonists and the emergence of a new type of actor in the arena of responsibilities: corporations.

2.2.1 Human Rights and the New Global Actor

Traditionally, the protective apparatus of human rights sought to meet the demands of the relationship between individuals and States, so that the process of internationalisation had as its perspective the creation of 'an international system of protection through which it became possible to hold the State accountable on the external level, when, internally, the competent bodies do not provide satisfactory responses to the protection of these rights'.[80] Therefore, the state duties of respect, protection and promotion of human rights by the States were endorsed,[81] moving individuals to the level of true subjects of international law—until then dedicated to State relations.[82]

Although the protective apparatus of the 'new' subjects of international law has expanded over the years and reached numerous *material*[83] specialities essential for protection, it is pertinent, for the purposes of this work, to understand the relationship between individuals—or rather the protection of these subjects in the international (and internal) sphere—and the new actors or non-formal subjects of international law. They are said to be non-formal since these subjects do not have (or had), *a priori,* legal capacity to conclude treaties and other international acts or even to have access to international courts.[84]

It is notorious that large companies or corporations, especially transnational ones, today exert strong economic power to the point of influencing political decisions, so

---

[80] Mazzuoli (2018), p. 66.

[81] Mazzuoli indicates provisions that, already in the UN Charter, made express reference to the respect, protection and promotion of human rights: Art. 1, Art. 13.1, Art. 55, Art. 56, Art. 62.2, Art. 68 and Art. 76. Mazzuoli (2018), p. 75.

[82] 'After the Second World War, the face of international society changed drastically, giving rise to a *new* international order from then on. Between the 17th and 19th centuries, states (mainly European) held, in an *exclusive* manner, the quality of subjects of Public International Law. After the twentieth century, this situation changes, with such states having to share this former *status* with other actors of international society [. . .]'. (Our translation). Mazzuoli (2013), p. 432.

[83] See, for example, the list of human rights issues/problems pointed out by the Office of the United Nations High Commissioner for Human Rights (OHCHR): OHCHR (2022). Topics. https://www.ohchr.org/en/issues/pages/listofissues.aspx. Accessed 1 Aug 2022.

[84] Mazzuoli points out that transnational companies present themselves today as non-formal subjects of Public International Law. Mazzuoli (2013), pp. 458–459.

that, within the contours of economic globalisation and the consequences to the internal scope (*v. supra*), nation-states are directed to negotiate with economic forces that transcend the national level and end up conditioning their investments to the acceptance of their values, their rules and their procedures.[85] José Eduardo Faria mentions, even, strategies of deregulation, delegalisation and deconstitutionalisation, which pave the way for an intricate articulation of socioeconomic systems and subsystems, with the expansion of the *lex mercatoria* in the internal environment of the States.[86]

At the end of the last century, Faria was already questioning the relationship between this scenario and the protection of human rights, especially because they are traditionally opposed to the State—that is, as a way to limit power in the individual sphere. Given this situation, how would individuals be protected in this new panorama where states are in crisis in the face of the transnationalisation of markets? In other words, the author questions: if human rights can only 'be instrumentalised through public power itself, how can they be effective at the moment when this same power is relativised by the phenomenon of globalisation?'[87]

This means to say that the idea of exclusive accountability of the State is no longer capable of responding to the problems that arise in a complex political-economic context, globalised, as is the current world order. In other words, if before the protection (whether positive or negative)[88] of human rights was driven only against States, in the current era of globalisation the distinguished role of companies in the protective sphere is called into question, that is, in the passive pole of responsibilities.

Globalisation has allowed the approximation between civilisations through the interdependence of capital flow, labour, technical knowledge and access to goods, services and materials. However, at the same time, the scenario of international exchange has fostered the formulation of a model of free market on a large scale, from which distinct social, economic and ethical consequences have emerged.[89] In this scenario, corporations,[90] especially those that

---

[85] Faria (1997), p. 47.

[86] Faria (1997), p. 47.

[87] Faria (1997), p. 48.

[88] In the publication '*Frequently Asked Questions on the Guiding Principles on Business and Human Rights*', the United Nations answered the question '*How are human rights relevant to business?*' informing the positive and negative aspects arising from business activity: 'it has long been recognised that businesses can have a profound impact on human rights. *This impact can be positive*, for example, by providing innovation and services that can *improve people's living standards* worldwide. *It can also be negative*, for example, *when business activities destroy people's livelihoods, exploit workers or displace communities*. Businesses can also be *complicit in human rights abuses committed by third parties*, including states—for example, if they conspire with security forces to suppress protests violently or provide information about their customers to states that use them to track and punish dissidents'. (our emphasis). United Nations (2014), pp. 4–5.

[89] Rivera (2017) Los desafíos de la globalización: reflexiones sobre la responsabilidad empresarial en materia de derechos humanos. In: Rivera (2017), pp. 36–37.

[90] '*Historians may look back at the 1990s as a "golden age" for the most recent wave of corporate globalisation. Multinational firms emerged robustly, in larger number and greater*

are transnational or multinational, by holding a significant portion of the international capital circulation, end up exerting broad economic (and political) power over other international subjects, particularly by acting as cardinal actors of direct foreign investments.[91]

Regarding the growing economic and political power of corporations, Sarah Anderson and John Cavanagh, from the *Institute for Policy* Studies, an NGO based in Washington, published (in 1996 and later in 2000) a study indicating that, of the hundred largest world economies of the time, 51 were companies and 49 were countries, with some corporations being larger even than several nations. They also demonstrated that the sales of each of the five largest companies were superior to the Gross Domestic Product (GDP) of 182 countries. They concluded that the 'broad liberalisation of trade and investment contributed to a climate in which the dominant companies are enjoying increasing levels of economic and political influence [. . .]'.[92]

Even today, the economic prominence of large corporations in relation to countries is discussed, highlighting that the ten largest companies in the world have a combined revenue greater than that of 180 poorest countries,[93] that the scale of the profits of the large corporations takes on a whole new meaning when compared to the GDP of many countries,[94] that some technology companies would be larger than many countries,[95] and that the net worth of large brands is superior to that of several nations.[96]

---

scale than ever before. They weaved together integrated spheres of transnational economic activity, subject to a single global strategic vision, operating, in real time, connected to and yet also transcending merely "national" economies and their "inter-national" transactions. Soon half of the world trade comprised "internal" transactions within networks of related corporate entities [. . .]'. Ruggie (2013), p. 15.

[91] 'In 2006 the developing countries attracted $380 billion of foreign direct investment'. Letnar Černič (2008), p. 72.

[92] Anderson and Cavanagh (2000), DC, p. 1.

[93] Data gathered by *Global Justice Now* from a direct comparison between the annual revenue of companies and the annual revenue of countries, according to the *CIA World Factbook 2015* and the *Fortune Global 500*. Global Justice Now (2021). The 10 biggest corporations make more money than most countries. https://www.globaljustice.org.uk/news/10-biggest-corporations-make-more-money-most-countries-world-combined/.

[94] For example, in 2017, Walmart's revenue was higher than Belgium's, Santander Bank's revenue was larger than Panama's GDP, Coca-Cola's revenue was larger than Bolivia's GDP, Facebook's revenue was larger than Serbia's, Apple's revenue was larger than Portugal's GDP, Volkswagen's revenue was larger than Chile's GDP, etc. Belinchón and Moynihan (2018) 25 giant companies that are bigger than entire countries. Business Insider España, 25 Jul. https://www.businessinsider.com/25-giant-companies-that-earn-more-than-entire-countries-2018-7.

[95] Comparing users and populations, Netflix would be larger than Russia, Amazon Prime Video would be the tenth largest country in the world, Spotify would be larger than Mexico and Japan, HBO Max is larger than the Netherlands, etc. MacKeeper (2021) How large would tech companies be if they were countries? MacKeeper.com, 13 Aug. https://mackeeper.com/blog/tech-giants-as-countries/.

[96] Comparing with the GDP of countries, Apple is richer ($2.2 trillion) than Italy ($2 trillion), Brazil ($2 trillion) and Canada ($1.8 trillion); Microsoft is richer ($1.8 trillion) than Russia

It happens that these large companies, inflated by new technologies, have started to direct their economic activities to various countries, operating globally through their subsidiaries and decentralising their offices at the multinational level, which became known as *global supply chains*.[97] This fact has brought new perspectives and challenges in the protection of human rights,[98] especially because, in the absence of a common legal framework for protection, companies, often supported by ideas of inherent risk to their activity and profit maximisation, take advantage of the weaknesses of the domestic rules of the recipient countries (*host states*) of their branches.[99]

Although the globalised economy and companies, as global axes of this reality, can support, directly or indirectly, a wide range of rights that make human life more tolerable, enjoyable and rewarding, some corporate practices, whether of multinational companies or not,[100] can simply erode the respect for these rights.[101]

($1.6 trillion), South Korea ($1.6 trillion) and Australia ($1.3 trillion); Amazon is richer ($1.6 trillion) than Spain ($1.3 trillion) and Mexico ($1.2 trillion). Cohen (2021) World's most valuable tech companies are richer than most countries. PCMag, 2 Apr. https://www.pcmag.com/news/worlds-most-valuable-tech-companies-are-richer-than-most-countries.

[97] 'In most sectors, large companies now rely on a range of contractors and suppliers in a variety of countries to produce and transport their products. Today's global supply chains link individual workers to large and small companies beyond national, political, and cultural borders. Companies generally do not own or operate the factories in which their products are produced and they may contract hundreds, sometimes thousands, of different suppliers annually'. (Our translation). Nolan (2016), p. 26.

[98] 'The accumulation of human rights issues and issues directly derived from business practices during the 1990s was not, of course, a coincidence. Instead, it was the result of the changing context of doing business in the post-Cold War global economy. The policies of liberalisation, deregulation, and privatisation of the Washington Consensus, which rapidly spread around the world during the late 1980s and 1990s, profoundly altered not only the size and structure of the global market, but also the power relations in the global political economy. In this ongoing process, states are losing some of their power to fully control social, economic, and even political processes, both globally and domestically. In this context, the effectiveness of the State as the sole protector of people's most basic rights has become questionable and the call to extend responsibility for human rights to non-state actors in general and in the private sphere, in particular, has become louder'. Wettstein (2012), p. 739–770.

[99] Piovesan and Gonzaga (2019), p. 15.

[100] It should be noted: 'This is not to suggest that the adverse impacts of companies' actions were restricted to multinational corporations. Indeed, rampant abuses, often undetected, occurred (and continue to occur) in companies of all kinds'. Institute for Human Rights and Business (2019), p. 10.

[101] Nolan (2016), pp. 23–24. The author also highlights that 'some companies are guilty of mistreating workers—in terms of pay, conditions and work environments; some pollute the environment in ways that have dramatic and serious effects far beyond their immediate surroundings; some discriminate against indigenous peoples, or certain ethnic or religious groups, or against women, or people with disabilities, or on grounds of sexuality; and some work alongside (or within) governments that commit serious human rights violations, such as in Nazi Germany and Apartheid South Africa and in many authoritarian and repressive states of the world today'. Nolan (2016). p. 25.

Thus, in the same path where globalisation has allowed these companies, especially from the global North, to enjoy the fruits of free international trade, individuals, populations and developing states in the global South face the adverse consequences of this action, so that cross-border business activity serves as a catalyst for violations[102] of human rights.[103]

This is because global integration at an economic level was not accompanied by complete integration, with legal instruments capable of curbing the negative aspects caused by this phenomenon. It is said that there is a *governance gap*,[104] or governance gap, because although the interaction between various legal regimes allowed companies to consolidate as entities with significant rights and prerogatives, global action was not accompanied by minimum obligations regarding the human rights of the communities in the places where these corporations began to operate.[105]

There is no doubt that, in this scenario, complex interactions emerged to encompass, on the one hand, companies and, on the other, the community and vulnerable groups,[106] to the point of significantly altering the dynamics of human rights, as the debate about their protection is no longer confined only to the matrix of individuals and the State and has begun to encompass the role played by corporations.

This also means, as Surya Deva explains, that the paradigm shift did not occur only in the relationship of 'right-duty bearers', but also in the nature of human rights violators[107], since the emergence of corporations on a global scale brought to light the insufficiency of traditional law (initially with international law and human rights treaties) to impose legal obligations on these private actors, as well as the difference in regulatory standards between countries (*home states* and *host states*) and the total absence of global standards applicable to companies.[108]

Indeed, it has always been questioned how the actions of corporations could be contained at an international level, especially because transnational corporations, in addition to not being globally regulated, often end up being subject to the legislation of the locality in which they operate. Moreover, even these legislations, when

[102] 'When can it be said that a company has violated human rights? The question can arise in three different situations: first, when the company itself is directly violating human rights; second, when a company aids or contributes to human rights violations committed by state agencies or other business entities; and third, when independent entities with which the company in question has a business relationship (i.e., subsidiaries and suppliers) violate rights. In each of these situations, the issue of "violation" necessarily arises in the context of the violation of an obligation. Therefore, the meaning of violation can be properly understood with reference to the nature and scope of companies' human rights obligations'. Deva (2012), p. 18.

[103] Letnar Černič (2008), p. 71.

[104] Ruggie (2013), p. 119.

[105] Rivera (2017, p. 37.

[106] Piovesan and Gonzaga (2019), p. 15.

[107] Deva (2012), p. 3.

[108] Rivera (2017), p. 37.

they prohibit abusive conduct, often end up not being implemented by States in many cases—either because they fail in this task, lack coercive capacity, fear the competitive consequences of doing so or because their leaders subordinate the public good in favour of private gain.[109]

In view of this reality, a new field of discussion began about the human costs of corporate globalisation. This topic brings to the fore not only the complex process of structural transformation, with its numerous interdisciplinary aspects,[110] but also the need for companies (regardless of the local, national or transnational nature of their operations) and their activities to be regulated more effectively, adopting, above all, a human rights perspective as the cardinal point for the development of a sustainable social and international order—in which all humanity enjoys all rights and freedoms.[111]

At this level, where there is no doubt about the inherent relationship between human rights and companies, numerous questions are raised to address the practical concerns of this interaction, especially because it has become evident that corporations are covered by the spectrum of responsibilities in terms of human rights.

In this sense, answers are being sought to some practical questions: 'What is the scope of this responsibility? What are the limits and potentialities of the international protective architecture in facing the challenge of boosting the role of companies in the field of human rights?'[112] Or even, 'How in a world of companies and States that maximise profit, jealously guarding their sovereign prerogatives, can multinational corporate conduct be regulated to prevent or mitigate such human costs?'[113]

2.2.2 *The Regulation of Corporate Activity at an International Level in Terms of Human Rights*

Although it has gained space in international debates in recent decades, the interface between business and human rights has not been a recent phenomenon.[114] It can be suggested that the *main thrust* of this relationship has changed over the years. Its transformations can be analysed in three major 'eras': the era of 'business

[109] Ruggie (2013), p. 16.

[110] '[. . .] that influences the enjoyment of civil, political, economic, social and cultural rights, including the right to development'. United Nations General Assembly (2007) Resolution 61/156: Globalisation and its consequences for the full enjoyment of all human rights.

[111] United Nations General Assembly (2007) Resolution 61/156: Globalisation and its consequences for the full enjoyment of all human rights, §43.

[112] Piovesan and Gonzaga (2019) pp. 11–28, p. 15.

[113] Ruggie (2013), p. 16.

[114] Institute for Human Rights and Business (2019). *Building a Movement: Reflections on the History and Future of Business and Human Rights*.

or human rights', the era of 'business *and* human rights' and the era of 'business *of* human rights'.[115]

Surya Deva[116] names the initial era as that of 'business *or* human rights', in which, in the free market economy, the only social responsibility of businesses is to maximise the profits of the *shareholders* (owners and shareholders),[117] thus, so to speak, a model of '*shareholder primacy*', without room for social purposes.

Although there is no clear starting or ending point of the 'eras'—as they all coexist in parallel—,[118] the next era is marked by the movement 'business *and* human rights'. It has its landmark in the early 1970s with United Nations studies on the impacts of transnational corporations on economic development and international relations,[119] as well as in the development and launch of *soft law* (or *non-binding instruments*)[120] norms on the responsibilities of multinational companies by the Organisation for Economic Co-operation and Development (OECD)[121] and the International Labour Organization (ILO).[122]

---

[115] Deva (2020), p. 1.

[116] Deva (2020), p. 2.

[117] The author recalls the words of the economist and professor at the University of Chicago, Friedman (1962), p. 2.

[118] Deva (2020), p.1.

[119] In 1974, the Commission for Transnational Corporations and the United Nations Centre for Transnational Corporations were established. However, with economic and political changes in the 1980s and 1990s, the Centre was abolished and its work was incorporated into the United Nations Conference on Trade and Development (UNCTAD). Since then, numerous research and documents have been produced, along with policy analysis and training support for developing countries. United Nations (2009).

[120] In a broad definition, *soft law* includes those instruments categorised as 'non-binding or voluntary resolutions and codes of conduct formulated and accepted by international and regional organisations, along with statements prepared by individuals or groups in a non-governmental capacity, but which intend to promote international principles. This would include, for example, codes of conduct developed not only at an international level, but also at a more micro level by multi-stakeholder groups that trust and profess to promote international rights'. Nolan (2013) In: Deva S, Bilchitz D (eds), p. 143.

[121] Although they did not have, at that time, the component of human rights and complaint mechanisms, the OECD Guidelines for Multinational Enterprises of 1976 were recommendations on responsible business conduct directed by governments to multinational companies operating *in or from* adhering countries. 'They provide non-binding principles and standards for responsible business conduct in a global context consistent with applicable laws and internationally recognised standards. The *Guidelines* are the only multilaterally agreed responsible business conduct code that governments have committed to promote'. OECD (2011) OECD *Guidelines for Multinational Enterprises*. OECD Publishing, Paris.

[122] The ILO Tripartite Declaration of Principles on Multinational Enterprises and Social Policy was first regulated and approved in 1977 and is now in its fifth edition (2017). It 'is the only ILO instrument that provides direct guidance to companies (multinational and national) on inclusive, responsible and sustainable social policies and work practices'. International Labour Organization (2021) Tripartite Declaration of Principles concerning Multinational Enterprises and Social Policy (MNE Declaration). https://www.ilo.org/empent/areas/mne-declaration/lang–en/index.htm.

The emerging debate moved beyond labour issues, which traditional studies were limited to, and began to focus on a broader investigation of the systematic relationship between businesses and human rights. This investigation sought to define and conceptualise this interaction, especially due to the need to extend responsibility for such rights to new international actors in the face of the loss of effectiveness of states in providing them as the sole protector.[123]

The rise of the era of 'business *and* human rights' was based on the development of standards (new *rules of the game*) to guide corporate behaviour. These standards were developed jointly by states, international organisations, multi-stakeholder groups and civil society organisations (CSOs),[124] as well as by associations of lawyers (*corporate legal accountability efforts*), who began to pursue corporate responsibility for human rights violations in court.[125]

Therefore, the prominence of the era 'business *and* human rights' over the era 'business *or* human rights' was established, and it can even be pointed out that there were four distinct phases in the United Nations' elevation of the theme.[126]

In the first phase, which lasted about two decades (1974–1992), the debate and disagreements revolved around the relationship 'rights *versus* responsibilities'. In the second, the discourse involved the issue of 'voluntariness *versus* binding regulations' and resulted in the *Draft Norms* of 2003[127] and the *Global Compact* of 2000[128]—both non-binding in nature. The third phase was marked by the mandate of Professor John Ruggie, which culminated in 2011 with the approval by the UN Human Rights Council of the thirty Guiding Principles on Business and Human Rights, established on three fundamental pillars: 'Protect, Respect and

---

[123] Wettstein (2012). pp. 739–770.

[124] Deva (2020). p. 3.

[125] Especially in the United States, with civil actions brought under the *Alien Tort Claims Act*. For example, cases brought by Holocaust survivors against Swiss banks and by residents of Myanmar for crimes of rape, forced labour and murders perpetrated by military units protecting the pipeline from Unocal. There are reported cases in the United Kingdom, such as Colombian farmers against BP, families from the Niger Delta against Shell, the responsibility of parent companies in relation to subsidiary company operations, etc. Institute for Human Rights and Business (2019), pp. 15–16.

[126] Deva (2020). p. 3.

[127] United Nations Economic and Social Council (2003) *Economic, Social and Cultural Rights: Draft Norms on the Responsibilities of Transnational Corporations and Other Business Enterprises With Regard to Human Rights*. UN Doc E/CN.4/Sub.2/2003/12, 30 May.

[128] For more details, Global Pact Brazil Network (2021) *The initiative*. https://www.pactoglobal.org.br/a-iniciativa. Also: 'In January 1999, the UN Secretary-General, Kofi Annan, brought the UN more proactively into business and the human rights arena with his call to business leaders to adhere to a UN Global Pact of values and principles to "give a human face to the global market." Company executives were invited to "embrace, support and implement a set of core values" articulated through nine principles that cover human rights, labour standards and environmental practices (the tenth principle of combating corruption was added in 2004); and forge partnerships

Remedy'.[129] Initiated in June 2014, the fourth phase is dedicated to the discussion of the duality of '*soft law* versus *hard law*', that is, the need to develop a legally binding international instrument to counter the norms of *soft law* or *non-binding*[130] regulations.

Specifically regarding the third phase outlined above, it is important to mention that, although Ruggie's Guiding Principles did not go unnoticed by critics, who pointed out the absence of mandatory compliance[131] (that is, the lack of enforceability or *enforcement* of the guiding principles towards companies),[132] they marked the consecration of the notion of corporate responsibility to respect human rights, including as an independent and complementary source to state protection duties.

---

with trade unions and NGOs to encourage greater inclusion and improve public trust in the global markets'. Institute for Human Rights and Business (2019), p. 18.

[129] The principles are based on three pillars (protect, respect and remedy): (i) the obligation of States to protect human rights against abuses committed by third parties; (ii) the independent responsibility of companies to respect, defend and not interfere with human rights, carrying out auditing processes (*due diligence*) to prevent violations and analyse their negative impacts iii) the duty of States to adopt appropriate measures to ensure that victims have access to an 'effective remedy'. United Nations High Commissioner for Human Rights (2011) *Guiding Principles on Business and Human Rights*. United Nations, New York/Geneva.

[130] Phase inaugurated by the creation, at the 26th session of the Human Rights Council, through Resolution 26/9, of the Open-ended intergovernmental working group on transnational corporations and other business enterprises with respect to human rights, whose mandate will be to draft an International Treaty to regulate, in International Human Rights Law, business activities. To date, the group has already released a third revised draft (*draft*), which served as the basis for substantive intergovernmental negotiations that were conducted at the seventh session (25 to 29 October 2021). For more details, see: United Nations (2021) *Open-ended Intergovernmental Working Group on Transnational Corporations and Other Business Enterprises with Respect to Human Rights*. UN, Geneva.

[131] '*Most importantly, while the principles provide some useful guidance to businesses interested in behaving responsibly, they also represent a woefully inadequate approach to business and human rights issues. That is because without any mechanism to ensure compliance or to measure implementation, they cannot actually require companies to do anything at all. Companies can reject the principles altogether without consequence—or publicly embrace them while doing absolutely nothing to put them into practice. The principles do not explicitly insist that governments regulate companies with the requisite scope and rigour; they also fail to push governments hard enough to ensure that companies respect human rights*'. Human Rights Watch (2013) *World Report 2013*, p. 44. https://www.hrw.org/world-report/2013#.

[132] Nolan exposes some specific criticisms, such as: the absence of a definition regarding the possibility or not of extraterritorial application of state norms that oblige companies to respect human rights; the flexibility and ambiguity in the language used to involve the commitments of companies in human rights, as the Principles would have given too much leeway, including many "shoulds" rather than "musts," which favours a mere "social expectation" rather than a legal obligation of respect; and the absence of a requirement for victims to have access to redress. Nolan (2016) Mapping the movement: the business and human rights regulatory framework. In: *Baumann-Pauly D, Nolan J (eds)*, p. 79.

This phase was (and still is) marked by a combination of co-regulatory mechanisms,[133] such as *guidelines* (directives) from multiple stakeholders (such as the ILO and OECD), declarations and codes of conduct adopted by corporations and state norms that incorporate international standards into their legal systems[134] in order to develop an environment and a business culture that values human rights.

By the stakeholders (companies, NGOs, unions, etc.), the discussions at this stage have evolved towards the development of standards, metrics and implementation mechanisms in order to give substantive content to corporate responsibilities[135]—especially in the face of protection gaps resulting from the inability of many governments and states to fulfil their human rights obligations.[136] As a result, there is a sharing (or transfer) of the 'post' of regulatory authority between states and non-state actors (a phenomenon that some have termed *re-regulation* or *regulatory renaissance).*[137]

However, it is worth noting the caveat presented by Surya Deva in his logic of 'eras' when mentioning the emergence of a new era, in which corporations and industry associations began to co-opt the language of human rights to serve their commercial interests, marking a significant shift towards the era of 'business *of* human rights'.[138] Although it may seem remarkable, the spectrum of this new era presents itself as a new market branch, which is becoming part of the problem in the process of solving another problem, especially due to the increasing corporate capture of state structures and the UN itself.[139]

This means, among other things, that corporations and industry associations are proactively controlling and shaping the discourse of 'business *and* human rights' in a way that aligns with their business objectives. In Deva's words, 'companies are

---

[133] Regarding all international initiatives on business and human rights, Nolan (2016), p. 80 ff.

[134] Regarding the latter, it is pertinent, for the purposes of this work (*v. infra*), to establish that such norms, for the most part, fail to achieve their protection objectives due to the absence of extraterritorial application.

[135] Nolan (2016), p. 67.

[136] '*Governments of countries that are home to the world's biggest and most powerful corporations—including the US, European nations, and emerging powers like Brazil and China—have consistently and inexcusably failed to scrutinise the actions of their companies when they go abroad. Most governments fall somewhere in between the extremes; few, if any, do all that they should*'. Human Rights Watch (2013) *World Report 2013*, p. 30.

[137] Nolan (2014), 7–23, pp. 8–9.

[138] 'A by-product of the UNGPs was the evolution of a new industry of corporate consulting on how to conduct due diligence in human rights'. Deva (2020), p. 5.

[139] '*The increasingly close partnership between the UN and the private sector gives corporations unprecedented access to influence all UN processes and agencies engaged with the BHR [Business and Human Rights] agenda. By way of comparison, it is worth noting here that the International Labour Organization (ILO) is a tripartite UN agency which engages not only states but also both employers and worker representatives—thus giving trade unions a counter-balancing role against corporate lobbying. However, other UN agencies have not institutionalised such a tripartite model, and giving certain non-governmental organisations (NGOs) consultative status is not the same thing as interacting with civil society on the same footing as states*'. Deva (2020), p. 7.

creating the public impression of being leaders in respecting human rights, but without bringing any fundamental changes to their current business models'.[140]

Among other issues, such an argument is based on the perception that, although almost all large companies are supporting the Principles Advisors, some of them continue to resist any attempt, at the national or international level, to impose binding obligations. Moreover, companies still advocate for a 'smart mix of regulation' that tends to mask the existing asymmetries of information, power, resources and influence among various stakeholders.[141]

By the way, Justine Nolan points to the flirtation, since the 1990s, of many companies with the notion of Corporate Social Responsibility (CSR). At the time, there was a notable expansion of corporate codes of conduct and experimentation in self-regulation by major brands (Nike, Disney, Gap, Reebok, Levi Strauss and Mattel). However, such modes of self-regulation 'were soon criticised for their lack of robustness, legitimacy, and effectiveness', notably because the instruments were developed with limited participation from stakeholders or, even, with few independent monitoring mechanisms in the assessment of corporate compliance with human rights and labour and environmental standards.[142]

Indeed, it is pertinent to have in perspective the discrepancies between CSR and the 'business and human rights' era. This is because, while the debate is inserted in the field of voluntariness and in the apolitical and private perception of corporations, CSR, throughout its development, proved to be conceptually incompatible with the nature of human rights, since these are rooted in legal and political conceptions. This means that human rights, seen as legal and political constructions or obligations,[143] became a 'blind spot' in the field of CSR, as it has a fundamentally voluntary approach and a moral obligation close to virtue and beneficence, or even philanthropy and charity.[144] Thus, the responsibility for

---

[140] Deva (2020), p. 7.

[141] *'Although smart mix is the favoured approach in the BHR field, it is puzzling that corporations want only binding rules in the domain of trade and investment. Moreover, one should ask a more fundamental question: the regulatory mix is smart for whom—for businesses or for rightsholders? Similarly, multistakeholderism is often employed to mask existing asymmetries of information, power, resources and influence among various stakeholders'.* Deva (2020), p.8.

[142] The author also highlights that, just as public criticism and media attention forced clothing and footwear companies in the 1990s, more recently attention has centred on the world's major electronics companies—such as Apple and Foxconn—and the working conditions in their supplier factories in Asia. Nolan (2016), pp. 27–28.

[143] 'The moral voluntarism of this type does not align with the focus on human rights issues. The language of rights is also the language of obligation. Rights and obligations are two sides of the same coin, otherwise, the idea of a right as a particularly strong normative claim would be empty and meaningless'. Wettstein (2016) In: Baumann-Pauly D, Nolan J (eds), p. 127.

[144] 'The conceptual incompatibility between CSR and human rights stems from two major problems, that of voluntariness and that of apolitical responsibility. The first presents itself in the sense that CSR has a character of "assumption of responsibility" or, still, of a "discretionary responsibility" of the corporation, which can act socially or not depending on its internal decisions. We speak of responsibility of "non-legal coercion," "optional moral," "supererogatory" and "imperfect obligations." Thus, the responsibility of human rights, being legal obligations,

human rights, being legal obligations without moral incursions, would be located outside the domain of CSR.[145]

With these caveats, it is essential that the tendencies of the 'business of human rights' era do not gain even more prominence; it is necessary, as Deva mentions,[146] to rescue the 'business and human rights' era from corporate capture. In this sense, the author mentions some steps to correct this phenomenon, speaking, among others,[147] about 'taking rights and rights holders seriously'.

In mentioning such a corrective step, it is proposed that the need for reflection on respecting rights implies that obligation holders have legally binding obligations and make informed decisions based on the common living experience of communities. It is also proposed that rights holders (*rightsholders*) should have the ability to seek effective solutions in case of violation, 'because rights without remedies do not mean much in practice'.[148] Thus, 'companies must have legally binding and enforceable human rights obligations as a precondition for doing business', without being, however, exclusively bound to the state model of enforcement.[149]

Thus, currently, in the delimitation of corporate responsibilities for human rights violations, there is a need for joint regulatory reinforcement between international soft law norms and state hard law regulations[150] as a way to change the nature of

---

without moral incursions, would be located outside the domain of CSR. The second problem stems from the fact that, while companies and their social responsibilities are located in the private domain, being interpreted apolitically, human rights, on the contrary, have traditionally been seen as tools to restrict and limit political power, having as recipients not companies, but governments and states'. Wettstein (2012), p. 739–770.

[145] '[. . .] CSR generally tends to adopt an isolated view of the corporation without having to engage extensively with the role of the State. That is, it defines corporate responsibilities largely without reference to the respective responsibilities of the State. Thus, conventional conceptions of CSR are based on a quite traditional approach of separating the public and private domains. While the State organises the public domain, companies and their respective social responsibilities are located directly in the private sphere. BHR, on the other hand, does not consider strong States guaranteed nor separates the public domain from the private. On the contrary, its objective is to extend corporate responsibility to a domain long seen as the exclusive responsibility of the State and, until now, in the public domain. From this perspective, it may not be surprising that CSR, with its clearly demarcated lines between the public and private domains, has not embraced BHR intuitively until very recently'. Wettstein (2016) p. 129.

[146] Deva (2020) pp. 10–14.

[147] It also mentions 'fundamental changes in the function, purpose and operations of companies' and 'allocation of costs of respect for human rights by companies', 'transforming the current development model' and 'creating a full range of incentives and disincentives'. Deva (2020) pp. 10–14.

[148] *The 'effectiveness of remedies should be judged from the perspective of rightsholders, remedial mechanisms should be responsive to the diverse experiences and expectations of rightsholders, remedies should be effective both in terms of process and outcome, and affected rightsholders should be able to seek a "bouquet of remedies" without any fear of victimisation'*. Deva (2020), p. 11.

[149] Deva (2020), p. 10.

[150] Regarding the interaction between norms of *soft law* and *hard law*, it is important to mention, as Nolan announces, that the growth of *soft law* initiatives. The issue of corporate responsibility in

the obligation and the possibility of developing a firmer basis for corporate legal responsibility.[151]

This comes, above all, from the criticism of the content of the documents formulated so far, especially because they lack a solid normative basis to guarantee an advanced level of law enforcement, translating into mere social expectations.[152]

Thus, although recent years have been marked by various instruments and the involvement of multiple stakeholders in the defence of human rights within the corporate sphere, criticisms are directed towards the fact that the regulatory mechanisms remain, for the most part, restricted and embedded in *soft law* norms and, if not toughened, will have limited effects in preventing future human rights violations by corporations.[153]

Broadly speaking, the voluntary nature of regulations aimed at companies has been seen as extremely problematic, firstly because instruments related to human rights protection deserve to be grounded in *hard law*—capable of conferring direct legal effects in national jurisdictions—and secondly because the proposed principles lack the credibility to provide greater sanctions for *non-compliance*, or rather, do not set strict terms to compel the implementation of compliance programmes by companies and, furthermore, the monitoring of their effectiveness by States.[154]

The fact is that responsibility, based on social expectations rather than constituting an effective obligation, implies the acceptance of a world in which companies are encouraged, but not obliged, to respect human rights.[155] In other words, the absence of impositions from open and modifiable structures generates uncertainties about the companies' genuine commitment to adopting the proposed voluntary principles. As Nolan points out, 'in its current format, corporate responsibility to respect incorporates a degree of fragility and flexibility', with the most urgent need in this field being the adoption of greater robustness and uniformity in the instruments, so that they not only encourage but compel corporations to, at the very least, respect human rights.[156]

Therefore, among the challenges associated with the instruments of the 'business *and* human rights' era is the practical implementation of normative guidelines. Hence, the need for States' involvement to complement and coerce companies to

relation to human rights has gained momentum due to the recognition of the failure of legal regulation (both internationally and domestically) to hold companies accountable. However, this does not mean that the aim of strengthening accountability through *hard law* will supersede the norms of *soft law*. On the contrary, such initiatives 'have become and will continue to be an important tool in the attempt to prevent and remedy corporate violations of human rights'. Nolan (2016), p. 83.

[151] Nolan (2016), p. 83.

[152] Nolan J (2014), pp. 8–9.

[153] Nolan (2016), p. 80.

[154] Prata and Martinelli (2018) In: Saad-Diniz E, Laurentiz, p. 200.

[155] Nolan (2013), p. 139.

[156] Nolan (2013), p. 140.

operate in a humanely oriented manner,[157] adhering to internationally recognised standards. In the words of Deva and Bilchitz, 'States have a critical role to play in the development of their constitutional and legislative structures to recognise such binding obligations'.[158]

Not surprisingly, it is mentioned that the practical implementation of such *soft law* principles requires regulation articulated in the form of *networked governance*, so that private regulatory mechanisms complement the traditional and formal role played by States in the protection of human rights. The spectrum of this protection network would then combine international and domestic, state and non-state (private) and *hard law* and *soft law* regulatory mechanisms.[159]

In the current scenario, this undoubtedly signifies a fundamental shift in the role of the State. If before it was incapable of regulating business activity alone,[160] it is now required to take responsibility for supervising and regulating companies' human rights practices,[161] notably because the protection standards of *soft law* norms tend to be more effective if they are mandatory in the form of true *law enforcement.*

The current situation presents itself, therefore, in the face of the inefficiency of private regulatory activities and *soft law* alone, and the incapacity of States to curb violations. Thus, to implement the guiding principles in practice, one needs to think about an articulation between the actors that uses private regulatory mechanisms endowed with the legal *enforcement* of States.

Therefore, the essentiality of constructing legal obligations that require due diligence in human rights, as well as the fulfilment of specific transparency reports imposed through national legislation, which will define the parameters to be required and sanctions applicable to violations, including on an extraterritorial basis, is discussed.[162]—as exemplified by the *US Foreign Corrupt Practices Act* (*see below*).

---

157 'The human approach has a more holistic view of the role of corporations in society. It considers corporations as an integral part of society; the role of companies, according to this view, is multifaceted, rather than being limited to efficient wealth creation'. Deva (2012), p. 11.

158 Deva and Bilchitz (eds) (2013), p. 25.

159 Nolan (2014), pp. 8–9.

160 Human Rights Watch (2013), p. 34.

161 'It is time for governments to pull their heads out of the sand, confront the problem they face, and accept their responsibility to supervise and regulate corporate human rights practices'. Human Rights Watch (2013). p. 30.

162 Nolan (2014), p. 19. Also: '*Beyond this, Human Rights Watch and others have argued that governments should regulate the human rights practices of their businesses, including by requiring them to carry out human rights due diligence activity and fulfil their human rights responsibilities under international law. Not only is this responsible policy, but it is supported by emerging norms of international law. In 2011, a meeting of international and human rights law experts adopted the Maastricht Principles on Extraterritorial Obligations of States in the area of Economic, Social and Cultural Rights. Among other things the Maastricht Principles describe the obligation of states to regulate non-state actors such as transnational corporations and other*

Thus, the evaluation of potential modifications that could contribute to the evolution of the human rights protection system has been proposed, analysing a normative structure that is compatible with the existence of open and flexible rules on one hand, and, on the other, with traditional state regulation, capable of constructing an integrated and coercively effective system in carrying out more forceful controls, such as the criminal liability of the legal entity.[163]

In this context, it is important to mention that the exact nature and scope of corporate obligations towards human rights are not yet well-defined.[164] However, 'human rights advocates in businesses need greater clarity and better data' to adopt a more robust human rights programme.[165] That is, it is necessary to overcome the confusion about what is specifically required of companies and what the best mechanisms are to substantially encourage them to respect human rights.[166]

According to a report published by the Economist Intelligence Unit (EIU) in 2015, the greatest current difficulty regarding the topic of human rights and business is the lack of understanding of what corporate responsibility means in practice. Although the majority of the 853 executives involved in the EIU's research broadly accepted that companies have a fundamental role in this area, they indicated the difficulty of implementing any profound practical change, especially given the confusion in understanding this complex topic.[167]

Thus, with the affirmation of the 'business *and* human rights' era and the consequent consolidation of the idea of corporate responsibility towards human rights, the debate has moved from the spectrum of 'whether' companies should engage with human rights to the level of 'how'. In the words of Justine Nolan, 'for many companies the question is no longer "do we have an obligation to address human rights?" Instead, it is "how to do it, at what cost and with whom do we collaborate to solve the problems that exist?"'[168]

Thus, it is essential to understand not only the regulation of corporate activity as established at the international level, including private regulatory efforts, but also the nature and limits of legal responsibilities in the face of human rights violations, notably to account for the construction of an integration model capable of providing more effective responses.

Therefore, this work aims to contribute to the debate about the understanding and delimitation of corporate responsibilities in matters of human rights, intending

---

business enterprises that are domiciled or closely linked in other ways to their territories'. Human Rights Watch (2013), p. 35.

163 Barrilari (2018), p. 195.

164 Baumann-Pauly and Posner (2016), p. 36.

165 Baumann-Pauly and Nolan (2016), p. 36.

166 Baumann-Pauly and Nolan (2016), p. 63.

167 The Economist Intelligence Unit (2015) The Road from Principles to Practice: Today's Challenges for Business in Respecting Human Rights. https://www.universal-rights.org/urg-policy-reports/the-road-from-principles-to-practice-todays-challenges-for-business-in-respecting-human-rights/.

168 Nolan (2016), p. 24.

to investigate the criminal limits involved in corporate activity that, in any case, are intertwined with potential violations.

Although it is not the scope of this work, it is important to mention that the current debate aims not only to understand the spectrum of responsibilities under the 'respect' pillar but also seeks grounds to extend corporate obligations under the argumentative mandate that companies, in addition to acting negatively by abstaining from violating rights, are also capable of providing rights, that is, of contributing positively to their realisation.[169]

This other focus is based on the criticisms formulated in relation to the Guiding Principles and their *human rights minimalism*[170]—in the sense that the obligations of corporations would have an exclusively negative focus, merely respecting human rights without any provision for a positive sphere in relation to companies—and reallocates a perspective of responsibility beyond *do no harm,* promoting a positive involvement of the company in the protection and realisation of rights.[171]

References

Books & Theses

Alcalá, H. N. (2013). El uso de las comunicaciones transjudiciales por parte de las jurisdicciones constitucionales em el derecho comparado y chileno. In A. Bogdandy von, M. Antoniazzi, & F. Piovesan (Eds.), *Estudos avançados de direitos humanos. Direitos humanos, democracia e integração jurídica: emergência de um novo direito público* (p. 265). Rio de Janeiro: Elsevier

Alves, J. A. L. (1994). *Os direitos humanos como tema global.* São Paulo: Perspectiva Publisher.

Anderson, S. & Cavanagh, J. (2000). *Top 200: The rise of corporate global power* (p. 1). Washington, DC: Institute for Policy Studies.

[169] The approach that the Special Representative of the Secretary-General for the issue of human rights and transnational corporations and other businesses adopts 'in relation to corporate responsibilities is also not logically coherent and comprehensive, since it does not engage adequately with the legal and moral normative basis of human rights. This basic failure, which is failing to articulate a clear moral normative approach that guides its work, also led to the erroneous conclusion that businesses only have negative obligations for the realisation of human rights. I have argued against these positions, which fundamentally limit the possibility of realising human rights and meeting some of the most urgent rights challenges in the twenty-first century Bilchitz (2013), p. 136.

[170] Expression by Wettstein. Wettstein (2012), 739–770.

[171] 'CSR can enrich the BHR perspective, mainly with regard to its focus on values and culture and its greater emphasis on positive responsibility. A closer integration of the two perspectives will lead to a broader description of corporate human rights responsibility as it is advanced, for example, by the Guiding Principles. In addition to the responsibility to respect, companies may also have the responsibility to contribute for the protection and realisation of rights'. Wettstein (2016), p. 136.

Baumann-Pauly, D., & Posner, M. (2016). Making the business case for human rights: an assessment. In D. Baumann-Pauly, & J. Nolan (Eds), *Business and human rights: From principles to practice* (p. 36). New York: Routledge.
Cançado Trindade, A. A. (2016). Apresentação. In F. Piovesan (org.), *Direitos humanos e o direito constitucional internacional* (16th, p. 71). São Paulo: Saraiva.
Canotilho, J. J. G. (2008). *"Brancosos" e a interconstitucionalidade*: itinerários dos discursos sobre a historicidade constitucional (2nd ed.). Almedina, Coimbra.
Carducci, M. & de Oliveira Mazzuoli, V. (2014). *Teoria tridimensional das integrações supra-nacionais: uma análise comparativa dos sistemas e modelos de integração da Europa e América Latina*. Editora Forense, Rio de Janeiro.
Chevallier, J. J. (2011). *El estado posmoderno* (trans: Pérez O) p. 241). Bogotá: Externado University of Colombia.
Cruz, P. M. (2007). SOBERANIA E SUPERAÇÃO DO ESTADO CONSTITUCIONAL MODERNO. J *Revista de Direitos e Garantias Fundamentais*. 2:69–98, 109.
Curso de direitos humanos, 5th rev, updated and expanded edn (pp. 68–69). São Paulo: Método Publisher.
Deva, S. (2020). From 'business or human rights' to 'business and human rights': what next? In S. Deva, & D. Birchall (Eds.), *Research handbook on human rights and business* (p. 1). Cheltenham: Edward Elgar.
Deva, S., & Bilchitz, D. (Eds.) (2013). *Human rights obligations of business: Beyond the corporate responsibility to respect?* (p. 25). London: Cambridge University Press.
Faria, J. E. (2010). The economic globalisation and its legal architecture: ten trends of contemporary law. *Paper presented at: Legal congress globalisation, risk and environment* (p. 1). University of Granada.
Ferrajoli, L. (2002). *A Soberania no Mundo Moderno* (p. 63). São Paulo: Martins Fontes Publisher.
Ferrajoli, L. (2014). *Derechos y garantías: La ley del más débil* (p. 16). Madrid: Trotta Publisher.
Ferrajoli, L. (2020). Il virus mette la globalizzazione con i piedi per terra. *Il Manifesto*, 17 de março de 2020.
Friedman, M. (1962). *Capitalism and Freedom* (p. 2). Chicago: University of Chicago Press.
Global Pact Brazil Network. (2021). *The initiative*. https://www.pactoglobal.org.br/a-iniciativa. Accessed April 2025.
Góngora-Mera, M. E. (2013). Interacciones y convergencias entre la corte interamericana de derechos humanos y los tribunales constitucionales nacionales: un enfoque coevolutivo. In A. Bogdandy von, M. Antoniazzi & F. Piovesan (Eds.), *Estudos avançados de direitos humanos. Direitos humanos, democracia e integração jurídica*: emergência de um novo direito público (p 312). Rio de Janeiro: Elsevier.
Häberle, P. (2007). *Estado constitucional cooperativo* (pp. 4–5). Renovar: Rio de Janeiro.
Häberle, P. (1997). *Hermenêutica constitucional: A sociedade aberta dos intérpretes da constituição: contribuição para a interpretação pluralista e "procedimental" da constituição*. In S. A. Fabris (Ed.), Porto Alegre.
Human Rights Watch. (2013). *World Report 2013* (p 44). https://www.hrw.org/world-report/2013#. Accessed April 2025.
Institute for Human Rights and Business. (2019). *Building a movement: Reflections on the history and future of business and human rights* (p. 10).
MacKeeper. (2021). How large would tech companies be if they were countries? MacKeeper.com, 13 Aug. https://mackeeper.com/blog/tech-giants-as-countries/. Accessed April 2025.
Mazzuoli de, V. O. (2013). *Curso de direito internacional público* (7th rev, updated and expanded edn, p. 432). São Paulo: Revista dos Tribunais.
Mazzuoli de, V. O. (2018). *Curso de direitos humanos* (5th rev, updated and expanded edn, pp. 68–69). São Paulo: Método Publisher.
Mazzuoli, V. O. (2013). *O controle jurisdicional da convencionalidade das leis* (3rd ed. rev., updated and expanded, p. 9). São Paulo: Revista dos Tribunais.

Neves, M. (2009). *Transconstitucionalismo* (pp. 22, 35, 122). São Paulo: Martins Fontes.
OECD. (2011). OECD *Guidelines for Multinational Enterprises*. Paris: OECD Publishing.
Piovesan, F. (2016). *Direitos humanos e o direito constitucional internacional* (16th edn (p. 406). São Paulo: Saraiva Publisher.
Piovesan, F., & Gonzaga, V. (2019). Empresas e direitos humanos: desafios e perspectivas à luz do direito internacional dos direitos humanos. *Revista do Tribunal Regional Federal da Primeira Região* 31(1):11–28, 15.
Prata, D., & Martinelli, S. (2018). *Empresas, direitos humanos e regulação: análise crítica dos princípios orientadores da ONU*. In E. Saad-Diniz, & V. Laurentiz (Eds.), *Corrupção, direitos humanos e empresas. Editora D'Plácido* (p. 200). Belo Horizonte.
Ribeiro, D., & Romancini, M. (2015). A teoria da interconstitucionalidade: uma análise com base na América Latina. *Revista de Direito Internacional*. 12(2):160–175, 164.
Rivera, H. C. (2017). Los desafíos de la globalización: reflexiones sobre la responsabilidad empresarial en materia de derechos humanos. In Instituto Interamericano de Derechos Humanos (org). *Derechos Humanos y Empresas: Reflexiones desde América Latina* (pp. 36–37). San José, Costa Rica: IIDH.
Ruggie, J. G. (2013). Just business: multinational corporations and human rights (p. 15). New York: W.W. Norton.
Wettstein, F. (2012). CSR and the debate on business and human rights: bridging the great divide. *Bus Ethics Q* 22(4):739–770.
Wettstein, F. (2016). From side show to main act: Can business and human rights save corporate responsibility? In D. Baumann-Pauly & J. Nolan (Eds.), *Business and human rights: From principles to practice*, New York: Routledge.

Book Chapters

Barrilari, C. (2018). Corrupção, empresas e direitos humanos: diálogo necessário. In E. Saad-Diniz, & V. V. Laurentiz (Eds.), *Corrupção, direitos humanos e empresas*. Belo Horizonte: D'Plácido Publisher.
Bilchitz, D. (2013). A chasm between 'is' and 'ought'? A critique of the normative foundations of the SRSG's Framework and the Guiding Principles. In S. Deva, & D. Bilchitz (Eds.), *Human rights obligations of business: beyond the corporate responsibility to respect?* Cambridge University Press, London, pp. 107–137.
Deva, S. (2012). *Regulating corporate human rights violations: humanizing business*. Routledge Research in Human Rights Law, New York.
Neves, M. (2017). From constitutionalism to transconstitutionalism: Beyond constitutional nationalism, cosmopolitan constitutional unity and fragmentary constitutional pluralism. In P. Blokker, & C. Thornhill (Eds.), *Sociological constitutionalism*. Cambridge: Cambridge University Press.
Nolan, J. (2013). The corporate responsibility to respect rights: Soft law or not law? In S. Deva, & D. Bilchitz (Eds.), *Human rights obligations of business: Beyond the corporate responsibility to respect?* London: Cambridge University Press.
Nolan, J. (2016). Mapping the movement: the business and human rights regulatory framework. In D. Baumann-Pauly, & J. Nolan (Eds.), *Business and human rights: From principles to practice*. Routledge: New York.
Ortega, R. N. (2013). Sobre la legitimidad democrática del diálogo entre jueces nacionales e internacionales tratándose de derechos fundamentales. In A. Bogdandy von, M. Antoniazzi & F. Piovesan (Eds.), *Estudos avançados de direitos humanos. Direitos humanos, democracia e integração jurídica*: emergência de um novo direito público. Rio de Janeiro: Elsevier.

Piovesan, F. (2013). Direitos humanos e diálogo jurisdicional no contexto latino-americano. In A. Bogdandy von, M. Antoniazzi, & F. Piovesan (Eds.), *Estudos avançados de direitos humanos*: Direitos humanos, democracia e integração jurídica: emergência de um novo direito público. Rio de Janeiro: Elsevier.

Prata, D., & Martinelli, S. (2018). Companies, human rights and regulation: Critical analysis of the UN guiding principles. In E. Saad-Diniz, & V. Laurentiz (Eds.), Corruption, *human rights and companies*. Belo Horizonte: Editora D'Plácido.

Journal and Article

Faria, J. E. (1997). Direitos humanos e globalização econômica: notas para uma discussão. *Revista Estudos Avançados*, 11(30):43–53, 47.

Ferrajoli, L. (2013). O futuro da democracia na Europa: direitos e poderes na economia global. *Revista Direitos Humanos e Democracia* 1(2):387–388.

Flores, J. H. (2002). Direitos humanos, interculturalidade e racionalidade resistência. (trans: Proner C). *Seqüência* 23(44):9–29, 21.

Letnar Černič, J. (2008). Corporate responsibility for human rights: a critical analysis of the OECD guidelines for multinational enterprises. *Hanse Law Rev*. 3(1):71–101, 72.

Mazzuoli de, V. O. (2013). *O controle jurisdicional da convencionalidade das leis*. 3rd ed. rev., updated and expanded. São Paulo: Review of the Tribunals.

Neves, M. (2005). A força simbólica dos direitos humanos. *Revista Eletrônica de Direito do Estado* 4:1–35.

Neves, M. (2014). (Não) Solucionando problemas constitucionais: transconstitucionalismo além de colisões. *Lua Nova* 93:201–232, 226.

Neves, M. (2014). (Não) Solucionando problemas constitucionais: transconstitucionalismo além de colisões. *Lua Nova*, *93*, 201–232.

Nolan, J. (2014). Refining the rules of the game: The corporate responsibility to respect human rights. *Utrecht J Int Eur Law* 30(78):7–23, 8–9

Piovesan, F. (2018). Declaração universal dos direitos humanos: desafios contemporâneos. *Revista de Direito Internacional e Direito Humanos da UFRJ*. 1(1):1–14, 1.

Tushnet, M. (2009). The inevitable globalisation of Constitutional Law. *Va J Int Law*. 49(4):985–1006, 986–989.

Legal Documents

Brazil. (1945). *Decree No. 19,841, of 22 October 1945. Promulgates the United Nations Charter*. http://www.planalto.gov.br/ccivil_03/decreto/1930-1949/d19841.htm

European Union. (2024). *Directive (EU) 2024/1760. Official Journal of the European Union*. https://eur-lex.europa.eu/eli/dir/2024/1760/oj

United Natins. (2009). *The UN and transnational corporations*. UN Briefing Note.

United Nations. (2021). *Open-ended intergovernmental working group on transnational corporations and other business enterprises with respect to human rights*. Geneva: UN.

United Nations Economic and Social Council. (2003). *Economic, social and cultural rights: Draft norms on the responsibilities of transnational corporations and other business enterprises with regard to human rights*. UN Doc E/CN.4/Sub.2/2003/12, 30 May.

United Nations Economic and Social Council. (2003). *Economic, social and cultural rights: Draft norms on the responsibilities of transnational corporations* (UN Doc E/CN.4/Sub.2/2003/12, 30 May).

United Nations General Assembly. (2007). *Resolution 61/156: Globalisation and its consequences for the full enjoyment of all human rights.*

United Nations General Assembly. (2007). **Resolution 61/156: Globalization and its consequences for the full enjoyment of all human rights*.*

United Nations High Commissioner for Human Rights. (2011). *Guiding principles on business and human rights*. United Nations.

Online Sources

Belinchón, F., & Moynihan, Q. (2018, July). *25 giant companies that are bigger than entire countries*. Business Insider España. https://www.businessinsider.com/25-giant-companies-that-earn-more-than-entire-countries-2018-7.

Cohen, J. (2021, April). *World's most valuable tech companies are richer than most countries.* PCMag. https://www.pcmag.com/news/worlds-most-valuable-tech-companies-are-richer-than-most-countries.

Global Justice Now. (2021). *10 biggest corporations make more money than most countries.* https://www.globaljustice.org.uk/news/10-biggest-corporations-make-more-money-most-countries-world-combined/.

Global Pact Brazil Network. (2021). *The initiative*. https://www.pactoglobal.org.br/a-iniciativa.

Human Rights Watch. (2013). *World report 2013*. https://www.hrw.org/world-report/2013#.

Institute for Human Rights and Business. (2019). *Building a movement: Reflections on the history and future of business and human rights.*

International Labour Organization. (2021). *Tripartite declaration of principles concerning multinational enterprises and social policy (MNE Declaration)*. https://www.ilo.org/empent/areas/mne-declaration/lang–en/index.htm.

MacKeeper. (2021, August). *How large would tech companies be if they were countries?* MacKeeper.com. https://mackeeper.com/blog/tech-giants-as-countries/.

OHCHR. (2022). *Topics*. https://www.ohchr.org/en/issues/pages/listofissues.aspx.

PCMag, Apr. https://www.pcmag.com/news/worlds-most-valuable-tech-companies-are-richer-than-most-countries.

The Economist Intelligence Unit. (2015). *The road from principles to practice: Today's challenges for business in respecting human rights*. https://www.universal-rights.org/urg-policy-reports/the-road-from-principles-to-practice-todays-challenges-for-business-in-respecting-human-rights/.

United Nations. (2009). *The UN and transnational corporations*. UN Briefing Note.

United Nations. (2014). *Frequently asked questions on the guiding principles on business and human rights*. United Nations.

United Nations. (2021). *Open-ended intergovernmental working group on transnational corporations*. UN.

Chapter 3
Corporate Corruption and Human Rights

There is no doubt about the progress made by the 'business *and* human rights' movement, which has brought a new paradigm to commercial practices and government policies, and whose successes should be celebrated. However, there remains a greater weight of unfulfilled potentialities and unmet responsibilities.[1]

The existence of corporate responsibility for human rights violations in its field of operation is evident, as seen in the overview presented in the previous section. However, the discussion about the limits and obligations, as well as the integration of regulatory models that combine state and non-state actors and instruments of *soft law* and *hard law,* is still unfinished and difficult. This situation already highlights the need to evaluate a normative structure capable of building an integrated and effective system that is compatible, on one hand, with the existence of open and flexible rules, and, on the other, with traditional state regulation[2]—a regulation that, in this work, is given by Criminal Law.

3.1 Corporations, Human Rights and Corruption: An Intersection

There are numerous difficulties involved in the theoretical evolution of the topic, for which there are still no definitive answers. Nevertheless, it is possible to verify that, despite the abundance of regulatory regimes aimed at delimiting their responsibility for human rights violations, we still witness a scenario of corporate

[1] Institute for Human Rights and Business (2019), p. 1.

[2] Barrilari (2018a) In: Saad-Diniz E, Laurentiz VV (eds), p. 195.

L. d. B. Ibarra Papa, *Prevention of Human Rights Violations in the Corporate Sphere*, IBCCrim Studies in Criminal Law, Human Rights and Criminology 1,
https://doi.org/10.1007/978-3-032-06213-0_3

impunity.[3] Therefore, there are reasons to note that corporations are difficult regulatory targets.[4]

In light of this reality, this work aims to contribute to the debate about corporate responsibility for human rights violations, noting especially how the anti-corruption framework can be an effective model for the construction of preventive mechanisms for human rights violations, beyond its mitigating measures for corporate crime.

This is because, as will be seen, the fight against corruption has led to the establishment of a new panorama of imposing corporate standards of compliance and integrity that can be used to confront human rights violations,[5] especially when considering the already pointed-out international influences (v. *supra*) that also aim at an approximation of corporate self-regulation with the protection of human rights.[6]

Although they are not clear and still require greater scientific cohesion, there are possible links between corruption, human rights and business.[7] From these, it can be pointed out that deviant business activity, based on illicit corrupt conduct—or on the crime of corruption in its various aspects—'has devastating consequences for the global economy, undermines the evolutionary forces of society as it indelibly compromises the proper interaction between State, capital and Law'.[8]

Although it is not a specific focus of this work, it is important to note that there is a connection between corruption and human rights,[9] and it is not singular or highly exceptional to envisage the negative relationship between them. In fact, scientific research has established a correlation in which corruption *per se* is inversely related to the realisation of human rights,[10] that more corrupt countries

[3] See, for example, the international movement *Stop corporate impunity*. Stop Corporate Impunity (2021) *Stop corporate impunity*. Available at: https://www.stopcorporateimpunity.org/?lang=pt-br.

[4] Deva presents a series of difficulties in the taxonomy of regulatory initiatives, indicating, in the end, a framework of regulatory inadequacy that would justify a reshuffle based on his *Integrated Theory of Regulation*. Deva (2012), p. 46.

[5] Here, we recall the research hypotheses: do companies violate human rights? Can *criminal compliance* be an effective tool to prevent crimes and human rights violations? Would the criminal liability of the legal entity contribute to improving the effectiveness of normative compliance?.

[6] Barrilari (2018b), p. 69.

[7] 'It seems that the scientific debate has not yet found greater cohesion between corruption, human rights and business. The search for convergences remains quite diluted in disciplinary debates, still lacking greater integration'. (Our translation) Saad-Diniz and Laurentiz (2018), p. 12.

[8] Barrilari (2018a), p. 188.

[9] *'In reality many links are evident'*, p. 3.

[10] 'The protection of human rights is inversely related to the presence of corruption in a society. This means that high levels of corruption in a society can prevent a state from fulfilling its duties to respect, protect and fulfil the human rights of its citizens. Corruption undermines the ability of states to comply with their human rights obligations because it erodes the capacity and trust of a state to provide public services GATHII, James Thuo. Defining the relationship between corruption and human rights. University of Pennsylvania Journal of International Law (2009) 31(125):125–202, p. 26.

tend to have low levels of protection and respect for human rights,[11] and also that both the violation of human rights and corruption undermine the political legitimacy of the State.[12]

Thus, given the correlation that presents itself between corruption and the violation of human rights,[13] despite the lack of causal evidence, it can be assumed, for methodological purposes, that corruption *itself* is a vector violating human rights, at least in the sense that it diverts resources that could be invested in their protection and realisation.

Therefore, what truly matters for the analysis of this work, in an effort to counter the scenario presented in the previous section, is the relationship between companies and corruption. In light of this, attention is drawn to corporate corruption in order to understand to what extent the penal system influences corporate delinquency, particularly to verify whether it is possible or not to jointly commit to the prevention of criminal legal goods and the protection of human rights.[14]

Currently, there is much discussion about the interaction between companies and corruption, and companies and human rights, without, however, integrating the three parameters under the same spectrum. If this were done, it would be possible to see that corruption, despite being associated with numerous rights violations,[15] could also serve as a paradigm for potential solutions.

Anita Ramasastry[16] observes that the prohibitions promoted by the United Nations Convention against Corruption, by guiding states to adopt criminal liability for legal entities that commit acts of corruption, could serve as a paradigm for the regulation of companies in the field of human rights. This is because, in the same way that the criminalisation of corrupt acts has induced corporations to act in a way to prevent illegal acts—through the implementation

[11] Among others, this was one of the conclusions reached in empirical research conducted through comparison of indicative data of corruption and human rights from 186 countries in the period from 1980 to 2004, presented at a meeting of the International Council on Human Rights. 'The statistical analysis shows that the most corrupt countries have worse records of human rights protection, even after controlling other explanatory variables, such as level of democracy, national income, population size, government consumption and regional control variables' Landman et al. (2007), p. 1.

[12] See more in: Rajagopal (1999) Corruption, legitimacy and human rights: the dialectic of the relationship. *Conn J Int Law* 14(2). 'It is undeniable, we believe, the very specific social harm of corruption. As it often lies at the exact intersection between organised crime and white-collar crime, it significantly weakens state authority, questions the administration of justice because it questions its exercise in relation to those whose behaviour should be the most impeccable, undermines the structures of institutions and democracies'. Santos (2003), pp. 963–991.

[13] '[. . .] capable of harming the development of citizens, in terms of the possibilities of effective social participation and, thus, the very maintenance of the democratic foundations of the State'. (Our translation). BECHARA, Ana Elisa Liberatore Silva. Corruption, political crisis and criminal law: the lessons that Brazil still needs to learn. *IBCCRIM Bulletin*, São Paulo, v. 25, n. 290, p. 05–07, Jan. 2017, p. 06.

[14] Sánchez (2019), p. 66.

[15] In depth: International Council on Human Rights Policy, (2009).

[16] Ramassastry (2013).

of *compliance* programmes—a global regulatory framework could be conceived that would radiate its parameters to the domestic field of each country with the adoption of national laws and regulations.

David Hess,[17] on the other hand, argues that if there were integration between a company's responsibility to combat corruption and its obligation to respect human rights, along with the adoption of a protective perspective of rights in anti-corruption measures, it would not only improve the performance of *compliance* programmes but also strengthen the moral foundations of companies. This would occur primarily because considering the violations caused by corruption would bring to corporate actors the social impact of their actions and would boost anti-corruption efforts beyond the primary motivation of neutralising the actions of *criminal law enforcement*.[18]

In this vein, the integration of the parameters (company, corruption and human rights) aims to instruct, in a more effective and coercive way, corporations to treat the fight against corruption as a necessary component to prevent human rights violations, since, under this perspective, participation in corrupt acts would resemble complicity in the violations caused by the state government.[19]

In this way, companies begin to play an active and preventive role through their *self-constitution*, betting on the development of *self-regulation* standards for business activity, with the provision of internal regulations and codes of ethical conduct and corresponding sanctions in case of non-compliance with defined obligations.[20]

It is certain that, initially, there is some difficulty in establishing points of contact between the objects. However, the demands of social development, especially those that take as a starting point an ethical and moral commitment beyond the purely private and economic scope, are conducive to reaching a new civilisational level in which companies assume commitments to fight corruption as one of the forms of guardianship of human rights.[21]

It is, therefore, about the possibility of considering self-regulatory mechanisms, both in the prevention of crimes and in the strengthening of corporate governance measures and corporate social responsibility, with the aim of being part of a cooperative business system for the prevention of widespread illegal acts,[22] including human rights violations.

In this context, it becomes feasible to defend an adequate means of protecting the impact of companies on human rights with the collaboration of Criminal Law, especially due to the current stage of expansion of the branch, which, with its internationalisation and readjustment of the legal sources of *soft law*,[23] brings to

[17] Hess (2017), p. 641–693.

[18] Hess (2017), pp. 641–693.

[19] Hess (2017), pp. 641–693.

[20] Silveira and Saad-Diniz (2015), p. 62.

[21] Barrilari (2018b), p. 90.

[22] Barrilari (2018b), p. 90.

[23] Silveira and Saad-Diniz (2015), p. 44.

light the tendency of dogmatics[24] to overcome traditional obstacles aimed at safeguarding individual interests and ex post damages, and to achieve a level of protection for collective legal goods and prevention of ex ante damages—especially in the sphere of economic crime.[25]

Evidently, corruption, due to its broad, general and transnational character, has solidified the need for standardised treatment, leading the international community—especially the UN and the Organisation for Economic Cooperation and Development (OECD)—to establish a series of integrity parameters that must be observed by the company as a provocation of a strong corporate stance against corruption in all its forms, favouring the adoption of mechanisms for the prevention of illicit acts[26]—the so-called *criminal compliance*.

In any case, the link between companies and corruption is not difficult to perceive; it is enough to pay attention to the corporate scandals accumulated from the last century to recent years. Such scandals can be seen both on a global scale and in local terms, with recent cases such as Odebrecht,[27] Petrobras[28] and Volkswagen,[29] which involve criminal corporate actions, including corruption of political agents, various frauds, payment of bribes, money laundering, etc.

Inserting companies into this context of illicit corporate activities does not seem, therefore, to be entirely inappropriate, especially when noting the rise of anti-corruption policies directed at legal entities: the *US Foreign Corrupt Practices Act* (FCPA) in the USA, the *UK Bribery Act* in the United Kingdom, and Law No. 12.846/2013 in Brazil. It is worth mentioning, also, the efforts of the global community in promoting international instruments to foster the assumption of state obligations to combat anti-corruption practices, even compelling states to insert

[24] Some argue it to be a 'specialised dogmatics of Criminal Law' (*Sonderstrafrechtsdogmatik*) for economic crimes or even, according to Wolfgang Naucke, 'economic-political crime'. Saad-Diniz (2018).

[25] Silveira and Saad-Diniz (2015), p. 26.

[26] Anti-corruption toolkits for business. Transparency International (2022) *Toolkits for business*. Available at: https://www.transparency.org/en/toolkits/business.

[27] See, in summary, the following news: Deutsch Welle (28 July 2020) The decline of Odebrecht. *Deutsch Welle*. Available at: https://www.dw.com/pt-br/o-ocaso-da-odebrecht/a-54350923. Accessed 20 Nov 2021; Desidério M (21 September 2018) 'Corruption in Odebrecht is the most organised in the history of capitalism'. *Exame*. Available at: https://exame.com/negocios/corrupcao-na-odebrecht-foi-a-mais-organizada-da-historia-do-capitalismo/.; Terra (22 December 2016) Odebrecht: understand the biggest bribery case in history. *Terra*. Available at: https://www.terra.com.br/noticias/brasil/odebrecht-entenda-o-maior-caso-de-suborno-da-historia,2ad4c9f40bf9d93e1b2fba08935c112cokpstq92.html.

[28] For more details, see: Ministério Público Federal (2021) *Understand the case*. Available at: https://www.mpf.mp.br/grandes-casos/lava-jato/entenda-o-caso.; Época (14 November 2014) *Everything you need to know about the Petrobras case* [12:19]. Available at: https://epoca.oglobo.globo.com/tempo/noticia/2014/09/tudo-para-entender-bo-caso-petrobrasb.html.

[29] For more details, see: Pozzi S (4 May 2018) *US sues former Volkswagen CEO over 'Dieselgate'* [22:44]. *El País*. Available at: https://brasil.elpais.com/noticias/caso-volkswagen/.

into their legal systems norms of corporate accountability for the practice of corruption and/or violation of human and fundamental rights.

Given this corporate implication, the current perception of the corruption phenomenon takes on multifactorial contours, so that its analysis permeates not only its relationship with human rights but also encompasses the economic market implications and the concepts of Criminal Law.[30] It is for no other reason that the assimilation of the idea of corruption surpasses, in current times, the mere provisions of the active and passive corruption offences of the Penal Code (PC), encompassing a new framework of confrontation, from the postulates of Economic Criminal Law[31] to the recent preventive approaches of compliance programmes.[32]

That being said, despite the numerous approaches that could be taken in analysing the topic, it is pertinent to note that this work will adopt a perspective from corporate criminal law or economic criminal law in order to understand the phenomenon of corruption from the perspective of corporate illegality and, in the end, to bring to light possible enhancements to counter potentially harmful corporate actions, such as criminal compliance and the criminal liability of legal entities (CLLE).

It is important to say that discussing the relationship between companies, human rights and corporate crime is a huge challenge, especially because each one has its own battles, so seeking methodological overlaps between them may seem somewhat intangible. However, in recent years, the doctrinal field has been making numerous efforts to demonstrate the convergence between the topics,[33] especially due to the gradual shift of the international criminal political agenda towards corporate crime.[34]

The degenerative relationship between the first two arcs—companies and human rights—as clarified in the previous section, leaves no doubt that corporations have a significant impact on contemporary society, particularly due to their direct and negative effects on human rights.

Therefore, in this section, we aim to build the bridges that allow us to understand corruption in relation to business or economic crimes, adopting perspectives

---

[30] Silveira (2014), p. 134.

[31] Especially when considering 'links between corruption and other forms of delinquency, particularly organised crime and economic corruption, including money laundering'. United Nations Office on Drugs and Crime (2007) *United Nations Convention against Corruption*. United Nations, Brasília.

[32] Silveira (2014), p. 134.

[33] Adán Nieto Martín proposes the emergence of a new sector within Economic Criminal Law whose objective is the protection of Human Rights and the provision of sanctions to multinational companies. Nieto Martín (2020) p. 137–172. Also: Crespo ED (2018), p. 11.

See also the recurrence of the theme in the discussions in the group of Young Penalists of the *International Association of Penal Law*, especially in the studies of the IV Symposium for Young Penalists held in São Paulo in 2014: International Association of Penal Law (2014) *Symposium for Young Penalists (4th)*: Regulation of abuse in the corporate scope. International Association of Penal Law, São Paulo.

[34] Saad-Diniz (2019), p. 14.

of policy and criminal dogmatics and corporate criminology as a way to assimilate the criminal phenomenon within corporate frameworks, especially as a way to establish the fundamental shields that will contribute to the critical analysis of *compliance* programmes and the CLLE.

In this way, we will seek to present the discussions from these perspectives, without denying that the convergence between the topics would require more precise and deeper incursions, which perhaps require greater methodological acuity, incompatible at the moment with the limits of this work.

3.1.1 Corruption and Corporations: Control From International Instruments

The current scenario increasingly shows the umbilical connection between corruption and companies, with corporate scandals[35] involving, for example, bribery, embezzlement,[36] influence peddling,[37] accounting and financial fraud,[38] irregular financing of political campaigns, fraud in bidding processes, use of frontmen, use of insider information and manipulation of capital markets,[39] among many other acts harmful to public interest.[40]

---

[35] See: The biggest corporate scandals of the twenty-first century. Estadão (9 November 2015) *Os maiores escândalos corporativos do século 21* [17:15]. Available at: https://economia.estadao.com.br/galerias/geral,os-maiores-escandalos-corporativos-do-seculo-21,22419.

[36] The most significant recent case in Brazil is, without doubt, the one investigated during Operation Car Wash, which indicated irregularities in the state-owned company Petrobras with the payment of bribes, kickbacks, embezzlement and money laundering involving from political parties to the main construction companies in the country. For more details, see: Understand the case. Ministério Público Federal (2021) *Entenda o caso*. Available at: https://www.mpf.mp.br/grandes-casos/lava-jato/entenda-o-caso.

[37] See, for example, Operation Daia: BENTES, VIANEY. Federal Police investigates corruption and influence trafficking at DNIT. Bentes V (24 August 2021) Operação Daia: Polícia Federal investiga corrupção e tráfico de influência no DNIT [08:35]. *CNN Brasil*. Available at: https://www.cnnbrasil.com.br/politica/policia-federal-investiga-corrupcao-e-trafico-de-influencia-no-dnit/.

[38] In the USA, there are several cases of great significance such as Enron, WorldCom and Lehman Brothers. Gara A (28 September 2015) The 10 biggest frauds in recent US history. *Forbes*. Available at: https://forbes.com.br/fotos/2015/09/10-maiores-fraudes-da-historia-recente-dos-estados-unidos/#foto3.

[39] See, for example, the case of OGX and Eike Batista: Federal Police will investigate Eike for fraud at OGX. Veja (18 April 2014) Polícia Federal investigará Eike por fraude na OGX [17:18]. *Veja*. Available at: https://veja.abril.com.br/economia/policia-federal-investigara-eike-por-fraude-na-ogx/.

[40] For instance, the case of Volkswagen's '*dieselgate*' which, in 2015, began to be investigated for installing *software* in its diesel cars to manipulate emission test results. For more details: 'Dieselgate': see how the Volkswagen scandal started and its consequences. G1 (23 September 2015) Escândalo da Volkswagen: veja o passo a passo do caso [15:48]. *G1*. Available at: http://g1.globo.com/carros/noticia/2015/09/escandalo-da-volkswagen-veja-o-passo-passo-do-caso.html.

Often, corrupt business activities are correlated with other harmful forms of delinquency, such as money laundering, smuggling, arms and drug trafficking and financing of terrorism.[41] Not to mention, also, the criminal actions that directly violate human rights, such as the environmental disasters experienced in Brazil in recent years.[42]

It is clear, therefore, that corruption, for some time now, has surpassed its traditional, typical characteristics and reached a new configurative level, no longer being limited only to a functional scope of Public Administration but also gaining space in commercial relations, including international ones.[43]

The current understanding of corruption reflects manifestations of a multifaceted and globalised phenomenon, with its specific scope also encompassing corruption in commercial activities within the private sector, clearly linking corruption to economic delinquency.[44]

The involvement of private actors in corrupt practices is a current reality, presenting a dual-faced criminological presence between white-collar crimes and organised crime,[45] requiring new forms of control to encompass not only the pursuit of individual responsibility of those involved but also of the legal entities in which, often, the events of corruption occur.[46]

---

[41] The international scenario is increasingly articulating in cooperation to combat corruption and money laundering, as well as the resulting organised crime. See, for example, FATF (2012) *International standards on combating money laundering and the financing of terrorism & proliferation: The FATF recommendations* (trans: Salles D). COAF, Brasília. Available at: https://www.fatf-gafi.org/media/fatf/documents/recommendations/pdfs/FATF-40-Rec-2012-Portuguese-GAFISUD.pdf.

See also Brazil's participation in international cooperation against organised crime and corruption: International cooperation is marked by the expansion of agreements against organised crime and corruption. Ministério da Justiça e Segurança Pública (2019) *[Title of specific content]*. Available at: https://www.justica.gov.br/news/collective-nitf-content-1554990835.08.

[42] See, for example, the direct relationship between corruption and the Brumadinho/MG disaster due to lack of inspection, as well as corrupt practices present in the ANM (National Mining Agency). See: Tribunal de Contas da União (2019) *Subsídios técnicos para a comissão externa do desastre de Brumadinho*. TCU, Brasília. Available at: https://portal.tcu.gov.br/data/files/40/80/3B/09/B7A1F6107AD96FE6F18818A8/Subsidios_tecnicos_comissao_externa_desastre_Brumadinho.pdf. Also, a report on the matter: Passarinho N (13 February 2019) *Fiscalização de barragens: órgão federal é o 2º mais exposto a fraudes e corrupção, diz TCU*. BBC News Brasil. Available at: https://www.bbc.com/portuguese/brasil-47211131.

[43] Silveira (2011), p. 414.

[44] Silveira (2011), p. 416.

[45] SANTOS (2003), pp. 963–991.

[46] 'Here, the cornerstone of the current penal concern: the validity and legitimacy of stipulating modal forms of business self-regulation and how these imply and chain effect, in penal effects, generating what is called *criminal compliance*'. (Our translation). Silveira and Saad-Diniz (2015), p. 62.

Considering that the phenomenon should be understood in different ways[47] and fought on many fronts,[48] it is in recent decades that the international movement against corruption has demonstrated the essential role of companies in the control front, as agents called upon to assume a share of responsibility. Although there are indications towards voluntary field measures, international instruments guide states 'to strengthen the sanctioning arsenal in case of non-compliance with the proposed measures, including the provision of criminal liability of the legal entity'.[49]

From the 1970s, due to the significant increase in transnational trade and, especially following the Watergate scandal in 1972, the United Nations turned its attention to the debate on corruption and presented, in Resolution 3.514 of 15/12/1972, 'measures against corrupt practices of transnationals and other corporations, their intermediaries and others involved'.[50] Since then, the importance of codes of conduct, the condemnation of all corrupt practices that violate laws and regulations in *host countries*, and the call for governments to adopt all necessary measures they deem relevant to the prevention of corrupt practices have been emphasised.

Still under the spotlight of the Watergate case, the American Congress approved, in 1977, the *Foreign Corrupt Practices Act (FCPA)*, legislation that prohibits the bribery of foreign public officials by American companies; that is, it makes illegal the payment of money or any undue advantage to foreign public officials in order to assist in obtaining or maintaining business.[51] With some amendments in 1978, this legislation took on an extraterritorial character, being applicable to non-American companies, which attracted the attention of the international community, especially after the conviction of large international corporations to pay million-dollar fines.[52]

Already recognised as a transnational phenomenon, the international scene became more sensitive to the issue of corruption, especially after the conclusion in 1996, within the Organization of American States (OAS), of the Inter-American Convention against Corruption,[53] which highlighted the purpose of promoting and strengthening the development, by each of the State Parties, of the necessary

[47] 'It can be said, therefore, that it is a polysemic expression, since it encompasses various meanings, both of a public and private nature. Along with sexual behaviours, others of an ethical, commercial or functional nature are added. Thus, corruption is not a legal concept in itself, but an object that varies according to the focus given to it by the observer who dwells on it'. (Our translation). JAPIASSÚ, Carlos Eduardo Adriano. pp. 321–343.

[48] Silveira (2011), p. 416.

[49] Barrilari (2018b).

[50] United Nations General Assembly (1976) *Measures against corrupt practices of transnational and other corporations, their intermediaries and others involved.* UN, Geneva. Available at: https://digitallibrary.un.org/record/189574.

[51] United States Department of Justice (2017) *Foreign Corrupt Practices Act.* Available at: https://www.justice.gov/criminal-fraud/foreign-corrupt-practices-act.

[52] For specific details about the legislation, see: Ferreira LV (2012/2013), pp. 98–101.

[53] Organization of American States (1996) *Inter-American Convention Against Corruption.* OAS, Caracas. Available at: http://www.oas.org/juridico/portuguese/treaties/b-58.htm.

mechanisms to prevent, detect, punish and eradicate corruption, accepting, in its Article 6,[54] a certain flexibility in the traditional concept of corruption.[55]

Subsequently, in 1997, the Organisation for Economic Co-operation and Development (OECD) promulgated the first global anti-corruption instrument: the Convention on Combating Bribery of Foreign Public Officials in International Business Transactions. Incorporated into Brazilian law by Decree No. 3,678 of 2000, it provided that it would be up to the State to establish, according to its laws, the criminal type of 'corruption of a foreign official'.[56]

In December 2000, through Resolution 55/61, the United Nations General Assembly created an International Committee for the formulation of a unique international instrument to combat corruption. Thus, in 2003, the same Assembly approved the United Nations Convention against Corruption, signed by most states, including Brazil, with the objectives (Art. 1) of promoting and strengthening measures to prevent and combat corruption more effectively and efficiently; promoting, facilitating and supporting international cooperation and technical assistance in the prevention and fight against corruption, including asset recovery; and promoting integrity, accountability and the proper management of public affairs and property.[57]

---

[54] 'This Convention applies to the following acts of corruption: **a.** the solicitation or acceptance, directly or indirectly, by a public official or a person who performs public functions, of any object of monetary value or other benefits such as gifts, favours, promises or advantages for himself or for another person or entity in exchange for the performance or omission of any act in the exercise of his public functions; **b.** the offer or grant, directly or indirectly, to a public official or a person who performs public functions, of any object of monetary value or other benefits such as gifts, favours, promises or advantages to that public official or another person or entity in exchange for the performance or omission of any act in the exercise of his public functions; **c.** the performance, by a public official or a person who performs public functions, of any act or omission in the exercise of his functions, in order to illicitly obtain benefits for himself or for a third party; **d.** The deliberate exploitation or concealment of assets derived from any of the acts referred to in this article; and **e**. the participation, as author, co-author, instigator, accomplice, sheltered or through any other means in the perpetration, in the attempt to perpetrate or in the association or conspiracy to perpetrate any of the acts referred to in this article'. (Our translation). Ibidem.

[55] Silveira (2011), p. 413.

[56] According to Art. 1, nos. 1 and 2, it is understood as 'offering, promising or giving any undue pecuniary advantage or of another nature, either directly or through intermediaries, to a foreign public official, for that official or for third parties, causing the action or omission of the official in the performance of his official duties, with the purpose of carrying out or hindering transactions or obtaining another illicit advantage in the conduct of international business'. It is also considered, in the Convention that 'complicity, including by incitement, aid or encouragement, or the authorisation of an act of corruption of a foreign public official is a criminal offence. The attempt and conspiracy to bribe a foreign public official will be criminal offences to the same extent as the attempt and conspiracy for corruption of a public official of that Party'. (Our translation). Brazil (2000) *Decree No. 3,678 of 30 November 2000: Promulgates the Convention on Combating Bribery of Foreign Public Officials in International Business Transactions*. Presidency of the Republic, Brasília. Available at: http://www.planalto.gov.br/ccivil_03/decreto/d3678.htm.

[57] United Nations Office on Drugs and Crime (2007) *United Nations Convention against Corruption*. United Nations, Brasília.

In addition, it is essential to highlight the role played by the Convention in the private sector (Art. 12) in the sense that each State should adopt measures to prevent corruption, as well as stipulate effective, proportionate and dissuasive civil, administrative or criminal sanctions in case of non-compliance with these measures. In addition to indicating criminal types to be regulated by the State Parties,[58] the document advocates the adoption of liability for legal entities for their participation in qualified crimes, which may assume a criminal, civil or administrative nature (Art. 26).

Other instruments that deserve mention are the Council of Europe's Conventions against Corruption,[59] with the Criminal Convention and the Civil Convention coming into force, respectively, in 2002 and 2003. The former,[60] in addition to describing criminal types of corruption, imposes criminal sanctions for both direct and indirect authors, as well as indicating that each State 'should adopt legislative and other measures that may be necessary to ensure that legal entities can be held accountable for criminal offences of active bribery, influence peddling and money laundering' (Art. 18).

The second,[61] like the first civil instrument capable of combating corruption, provides for the definition of rules for repairing the damage resulting from acts of corruption, indicating, therefore, that States establish 'effective solutions for people who have suffered damage as a result of acts of corruption, so that they can defend their rights and interests, including the possibility of obtaining compensation for damages' (Art. 1).

Under the influence of these international instruments, the United Kingdom enacted the *United Kingdom Bribery Act* (UKBA),[62] which came into force in 2011 with the aim of preventing corruption, both domestic and international, through criminal and administrative implications against individuals and legal entities that commit bribery offences.

Particularly, it is pertinent to investigate the influences that international instruments have on Brazilian reality, especially after the insertion of their provisions into the domestic legal system, it being certain that the three most

---

[58] It indicates, for example, bribery of national public officials (Art. 15), bribery of foreign public officials and officials of international public organisations (Art. 16), embezzlement, misappropriation or other forms of diversion of property by a public official (Art. 17), trafficking in influence (Art. 18), abuse of functions (Art. 19), illicit enrichment (Art. 20), bribery in the private sector (Art. 21), embezzlement or misappropriation of property in the private sector (Art. 22) and laundering of the proceeds of crime (Art. 23). United Nations Office on Drugs and Crime (2007).

[59] In 1999, GRECO (Group of States against Corruption) was established, whose objective is to ensure respect for both Conventions of the Council of Europe, as well as to develop effective measures for a better effectiveness in the fight against corruption.

[60] Council of Europe (1999) *Criminal Law Convention on Corruption* (European Treaty Series No. 173). Council of Europe, Strasbourg. Available at: https://rm.coe.int/168007f3f5.

[61] Council of Europe (1999) *Civil Law Convention on Corruption* (European Treaty Series No. 174). Council of Europe, Strasbourg. Available at: https://rm.coe.int/168007f3f6.

[62] United Kingdom (2010) *Bribery Act 2010*. Available at: https://www.legislation.gov.uk/ukpga/2010/23/contents.

relevant instruments of protection against corruption, adopted by the OAS,[63] OECD[64] and UN, were approved, ratified and promulgated by Brazil.

Especially, it is worth noting that the United Nations Convention was approved by Legislative Decree No. 348 of 2005 and promulgated in January 2006 by Decree No. 5,687 of 2006,[65] inserting a series of preventive and repressive measures, directed even to the private sector,[66] with the aim of 'safeguarding the integrity of private activities, for the honourable and correct exercise of commercial activities, for the prevention of conflicts of interest, as well as for the promotion of the use of good commercial practices [. . .]'.[67]

Regarding the criminal liability of the legal entity, as already mentioned, the Convention does not impose its adoption; however, it guides that each State use the necessary measures, in accordance with the possibility or not of its legal system. In the case of Brazil, the legal system, since the Constitution of 1988, conceives the

---

[63] Brazil (2002) *Decree No. 4,410 of 7 October 2002: Promulgates the Inter-American Convention against Corruption (29 March 1996) with reservation for Article XI, paragraph 1(c)*. Presidency of the Republic, Brasília. Available at: http://www.planalto.gov.br/ccivil_03/decreto/2002/d4410.htm.

[64] Brazil (2000) *Decree No. 3,678 of 30 November 2000: Promulgates the Convention on Combating Bribery of Foreign Public Officials in International Business Transactions (concluded in Paris, 17 December 1997)*. Presidency of the Republic, Brasília. Available at: http://www.planalto.gov.br/ccivil_03/decreto/d3678.htm.

[65] Brazil (2006) *Decree No. 5,687 of 31 January 2006: Promulgates the United Nations Convention against Corruption (adopted 31 October 2003)*. Presidency of the Republic, Brasília. Available at: http://www.planalto.gov.br/ccivil_03/_ato2004.

[66] Decree No. 5,687/06, Art. 12—Private Sector: '1. Each State Party, in accordance with the fundamental principles of its domestic law, shall adopt measures to prevent corruption and improve accounting and auditing standards in the private sector, as well as, when appropriate, provide for effective, proportionate and dissuasive civil, administrative or criminal sanctions in case of non-compliance with these measures. 2. The measures to be adopted to achieve these ends may include, among other things: (a) Promoting cooperation between law enforcement agencies and relevant private entities; (b) Promoting the formulation of standards and procedures aimed at safeguarding the integrity of relevant private entities, including codes of conduct for the proper, honourable and due exercise of commercial activities and all relevant professions and for the prevention of conflicts of interest, as well as for the promotion of the use of good business practices among companies and the contractual relations of companies with the State; (c) Promoting transparency among private entities, including, where appropriate, measures relating to the identification of legal and natural persons involved in the establishment and management of companies; (d) Preventing the misuse of procedures that regulate private entities, including procedures relating to the granting of subsidies and licences by public authorities for commercial activities; (e) Preventing conflicts of interest by imposing appropriate restrictions, for a reasonable period, on the professional activities of former public officials or on the hiring of public officials by the private sector after their resignation or retirement when these activities or this hiring are directly related to the functions performed or supervised by these public officials during their tenure in office; (f) Ensuring that private companies, taking into account their structure and size, have sufficient internal accounting controls to help prevent and detect acts of corruption and that the accounts and financial statements required of these private companies are subject to appropriate auditing and certification procedures [. . .]'. (Our translation). Brazil (2006).

[67] Barrilari (2018b), p. 76.

CLLE as a reality, especially through the provisions of Arts. 225, §3º[68] and 173, §5º[69]—the latter with implicit provision and still without regulation.

Regarding the guidelines and commitments given by the OAS Inter-American Convention, Brazil approved Law No. 10,467/2002, which amends the Penal Code to define who will be considered a foreign public official for criminal purposes and to typify passive corruption and influence peddling in international commercial transactions.

In addition, internal measures were adopted to combat corruption and money laundering with the creation and structuring of the National Strategy for Combating Corruption and Money Laundering (ENCCLA)[70] in 2003, which culminated in the creation of the National Training and Capacity-Building Programme for Combating Corruption and Money Laundering (PNLD) and in the drafting of the preliminary projects that resulted in the classification of criminal organisations, illicit enrichment and the definition of terrorism and its financing.

In turn, the Money Laundering Law (Law No. 9.613/1998) and the amendments introduced by Law No. 12.683/2012 present various criminal types and their respective sanctions linked to laundering, concealment or dissimulation of assets, rights and values originating, directly or indirectly, from criminal offence, as well as mechanisms for prosecution, processing and judgement.

Under the clear influence of international instruments, in 2013 the commonly called Anti-Corruption Law or Clean Company Law (Law No. 12.846/2013) was approved. This law provides that legal entities, in cases of the practice of illicit acts, in their interest or benefit, contrary to the national or foreign administration, can be held objectively, administratively and civilly responsible. They may be sanctioned (Art. 6), either in isolation or concomitantly, by means of: (a) a fine, in the amount of 0.1% to 20% of the gross turnover of the last fiscal year prior to the initiation of the administrative process or, in the impossibility of this calculation, from £6,000.00 to £60,000,000.00; and (b) the extraordinary publication of the

[68] 'Art. 225. Everyone has the right to an ecologically balanced environment, a common good of the people and essential to a healthy quality of life, imposing on the Public Power and the community the duty to defend and preserve it for present and future generations. [. . .] § 3º The conducts and activities considered harmful to the environment will subject the offenders, individuals or legal entities, to criminal and administrative sanctions, regardless of the obligation to repair the damages caused'. BRAZIL. Constitution (1988). Brazil (1988) *Constitution of the Federative Republic of Brazil*. Presidency of the Republic, Brasília. Available at: http://www.planalto.gov.br/ccivil_03/Constituicao/Constituicao.htm. Accessed April 2025.

[69] 'Art. 173. Except for the cases provided for in this Constitution, the direct exploitation of economic activity by the State will only be permitted when necessary for the imperatives of national security or relevant collective interest, as defined by law. [. . .] §5º The law, without prejudice to the individual responsibility of the directors of the legal entity, will establish its responsibility, subjecting it to punishments compatible with its nature, in acts committed against the economic and financial order and against the popular economy'. Brazil (1988).

[70] It consists of the coordination of public bodies, entities and civil society, which work in the prevention and fight against corruption and money laundering. See more at: National Strategy for Combating Corruption and Money Laundering (ENCCLA).

condemnatory decision, at the company's expense, through widely circulated communication means, in the commercial establishment itself, as well as on the company's website.

Furthermore, regardless of administrative liability, the legislation provides for the judicial liability of offending legal entities, foreseeing (Art. 19) the sanctions of: (i) forfeiture of assets, rights or values that represent advantage or profit directly or indirectly obtained from the infraction, except for the rights of the injured party or third party in good faith; (ii) suspension or partial interdiction of their activities; (iii) compulsory dissolution of the legal entity; and (iv) prohibition of receiving incentives, subsidies, grants, donations or loans from public bodies or entities and from public or government-controlled financial institutions for a minimum period of 1 year and a maximum of 5 years.

In addition, a significant and innovative point of the anti-corruption legislation and its specific regulation (Decree No. 8,420/2015) is the provision and valuation of preventive mechanisms, giving notoriety and relevance to *compliance* and integrity programmes, notably as an element capable of reducing any sanctions applied based on the objective liability of the legal entity (Art. 18, V, of Decree No. 8,420/2015).

Lastly, and most recently, in 2019, the federal government presented the so-called 'Anti-Crime Package', whose project contained a set of measures against corruption, organised crime and crimes committed with serious violence to the person, with amendments to various legislations. In December of the same year, the project was approved, with reservations, by the National Congress and sanctioned, with vetoes, by the Presidency of the Republic, thus inaugurating Law No. 13.964/2019.[71]

Envisioning the international scenario and its influence on the Brazilian legal system, especially under the criminal legislator, there is no doubt that the fight against corruption has been a topic of deep national preference, prompting political-criminal and theoretical efforts to validate the best use of the topic and its implications.

Despite Brazilian legislation intending to advance in terms of combating corruption and criminality arising from corporations, the current situation is not devoid of critical contributions, from which pertinent reflections can be drawn for the formulation of this work regarding the role of Criminal Law in understanding and forming effective preventive mechanisms.

In recent decades, following a trend of international harmonisation and internationalisation of Criminal Law, Brazil has tried, with the infiltration of transnational norms and rearrangement of the system of sources of Criminal Law,[72] to improve the configuration of corruption control mechanisms, with influence,

[71] Cunha (2017), pp. 131–177.

[72] 'Navarro Dolmestch mentions that globalisation, as an economic phenomenon, is characterised by the creation, on a global scale, of exchange networks generating a true and new world order. This also reflects in Law, especially in legislative production. Therefore—he states—, within a globalised legal perspective, although the decisions of the legislative process broadly occur

especially, from *soft law* norms, oriented particularly by international organisations such as the OECD and the Financial Action Task Force (FATF).

Initially, it should be noted, regarding this globalising trend, the risk that presents itself in relation to the distortion of Criminal Law. This conception of transnational integration—often based on economic premises—ends up disregarding the inherent difficulties of the relationship between norms and principles of different spheres (national and international), the complex interaction between different cultures and legal systems, and the consequent interlegality[73] resulting from the approximation between *hard law* and *soft law*.[74]

Secondly, the trend related to transnational Criminal Law, with adherence to significant criminal determinations arising from *soft law,* ended up adopting the prevalence of 'Criminal Law under the prism of an ideal of repression, increasingly rigorous and supposedly effective, at the expense of a deeper reflection on the effectiveness of preventive control measures of the phenomenon'.[75]

The processing and trial of the largest corruption cases in Brazil's recent history—Mensalão and Operation Car Wash—are examples of this, as, despite entailing the intensification of punitive state intervention and the construction of an anti-corruption

---

within the borders of a specific country by their respective national parliaments, they are not reflections of the aspirations of local actors. This *transnationalisation of the legal regulation of the nation-state*, undoubtedly shakes the very system of sources of Law, as well as the principle of legality itself'. (Our translation). Silveira and Saad-Diniz (2015) p. 41. (our emphasis). At another moment: 'Indeed, from a criminal economic perspective, the path has been paved, basically, as Viada puts it, by informal influences, and not necessarily of obligatory linkage, strongly influenced by the *soft law*. Note that the 'modern' Criminal Law, pointed out embryonically by Hassemer in the late 1980s and early 1990s, which would oppose the Criminal Law of the Enlightenment, seems to distinguish itself from this also in its sources, precisely because it seeks the necessary response to a phenomenon resulting from globalisation itself, that is, to supra-individual crimes (of which economic crimes are part). The search for *standards* minimum security shouted by globalisation ends up fostering a standardisation of the criminal system itself, and from there we see an increasingly frequent, recourse to the use of *soft law'*. (Our translation). Silveira and Saad-Diniz (2015), p. 44.

[73] Regarding the term interlegality: '[...] globalisation causes a real decrease in the relevance of national criminal laws in the face of a political pluralism formed by legal systems of various levels, which interact with each other in an exchange process. Such pluralism is not only formed by variations between sub-state and supra-state systems, but also encompasses the influence of new agents, which appear as international organisations, *lobbies*, non-governmental organisations and, notably, the influence of national rights of more powerful states (such as the United States of America) against the Criminal Laws of other countries. This becomes absolutely clear, for example, when we observe the pressure exerted by those countries with regard to anti-corruption legislation models, using as a background example their own 1977 law, known as *Foreign Corrupt Practices Act'*. (Our translation). Silveira and Saad-Diniz (2015), p. 51.

[74] Bechara AEL (2020) (1). Also, 'the influence of *soft law* in Criminal Law, as a supra-ordinary source, can be understood as the most worrying facet of today's transnational Criminal Law. Its presence, from the 1980s, completely changed the criminal landscape, as it shows itself as an atypical source of legislative production, thus assuming, a managerial role in relation to the mentioned second working group, in relation to specific crimes, here seen, particularly, under the aegis of the economic order'. (Our translation). Silveira and Saad-Diniz (2015), p. 54.

[75] Bechara AEL (2020).

culture, they overlooked the weakness of Criminal Law as a single effective control mechanism, mainly due to the lack of coordination with other formal spheres and the low yield in preventing new corruption events.[76]

In the words of Ana Elisa Liberatore S. Bechara,[77] it means that even after the advances achieved by such cases, it is clear that 'the repression of involved in the criminal sphere does not imply, in itself, systemic changes that prevent the occurrence of new episodes of corruption'. In other words, 'although criminal intervention is traditionally affirmed as the primary means of combating corruption [. . .] it is important to emphasise that criminal law always arrives deficiently and excessively late', so that 'the key to effectively combating corruption is not in punishment (although this should also exist), but rather in prevention'.

The criticism, therefore, points to the a priori adoption of control mechanisms derived from international regulations under the justification of an alleged need to respond more effectively to anti-corruption social demands, without presenting, however, the compatibility matrices with the Brazilian legal system, in such a way that, 'from the point of view of efficiency, criminal law is losing its fundamental character of *ultima ratio,* to become progressively one—perhaps even the main one—among several equivalent mechanisms of government intervention'.[78]

In this context, one can explore the content, legitimacy and the effects resulting from the choices of Brazilian criminal policy in controlling corruption through an excessively (and, perhaps, exclusively) repressive criminal law, notably influenced by the transnationalisation of legal regulation, in order to ascertain to what extent the dictates of this 'new criminal law' are justifiable in pointing out the presence of the institutions of *criminal compliance* and CLLE in the legal system.

Questions that will be examined below.

3.1.2 The Criminal Expansion and the 'New' Criminal Law in the Era of Compliance

Regarding the relationship between companies and human rights violations, it is inevitable to keep in perspective the 'set of legal norms that describe and combine sanctions for transgressions committed in the name or for the benefit of a business

[76] Bechara AELS (2017) Corrupção, crise política e direito penal: as lições que o Brasil ainda precisa aprender. *Boletim IBCCRIM* 25(290):5–7.

[77] Bechara AELS (2017).

[78] 'The need for a criminal assessment is replaced by the idea of agility in solving issues, going against the criminal and the procedural principles that underpin the democratic state governed by the rule of law. The protection of the individual is then relativised when compared to the need for superior protection of the so-called "common interest"; this is a virtually empty general concept, used to justify any type of excessive criminal intervention'. (Our translation). Bechara AEL (2020).

organisation',[79] notably called Business Criminal Law. However, one cannot lose sight of the relationship of this branch to the larger spectrum of Economic Criminal Law, which, for the most part, has collective entities as its main agent—so that the concepts can be used with equivalent meaning.[80]

Therefore, Business Criminal Law is a reflection of a larger phenomenon from which it cannot be dissociated: Economic Criminal Law (ECL).

In this scenario, it is necessary to quickly outline the foundational aspects of this branch of law that, stemming from new criminological contributions in the 1970s–1980s, began to draw the attention of criminal theory to criminality within the business world, with the company itself being the main agent, understood, in broad terms, as an entrepreneurial activity involving the production, elaboration and marketing of products, as well as the provision of services.[81]

As a great exponent of ECL, Klaus Tiedemann points out two conceptions or concepts of this branch of law: one in a strict sense and another in a broad sense. The first one is the protection of legal goods constituted by the set of the state economic order, that is, the national economy as a supra-individual value to be protected. The second encompasses a larger concept of economic crimes, forming the set of legal-criminal norms in the protection of the legal regulation of production, distribution and consumption of goods and services. While the first is aimed at collective protection, e.g. fiscal crimes and money laundering, the second visualises the supra-individual protection of the economy through the protection of the individual, the consumer or the investor, for example.[82]

There are several phenomena and factors that gave rise to and fostered the emergence of the discussions that permeate the ECL.[83] One can point to the increase—inherent to globalisation—of commercial and financial relations and the consequent expansion of the criminological reference in order to encompass the abuses *in* and *of* the market related to business economic matters,[84] especially in the face of the ever-increasing power of multinationals. Not to mention, moreover, that the intensification of economic globalisation and the consequent opening of international markets significantly altered the profile of international criminal policy, since,

---

[79] Souza (2021), p. 24.

[80] Referring to the classic study '*The concept of economic law, of economic criminal law and of economic crime*' by Professor Klaus Tiedemann, it is mentioned that 'not everything within the scope of Economic Criminal Law is developed by a company [. . .], but it can be said that the most important part of it corresponds to this'. (Our translation). Ibidem, p. 24.

[81] Tiedemann (2009), p. 53.

[82] Tiedemann (1985), pp. 18–19.

[83] Although this work has in perspective the legitimacy of this scientific branch, the criticisms regarding the expansion of Criminal Law, pointed out, especially, by the Frankfurt School, having Wilfrid Hassemer as the main exponent of the 'Intervention Law' and 'Sanctioning Administrative Law', are not ignored.

[84] Souza (2011), p. 106.

if before priority was given to traditional criminality, from globalisation the relevance gradually shifted to corporate criminality.[85]

As seen in the previous section, globalisation, among other numerous dimensions,[86] brought about the inflation of business markets, especially beyond national borders, giving the scenario of the 'new planetary power' even more complex contours, as there is no 'global society, nor strong international organisations, and even less, a global state' to confront this 'global economic power'.[87] For this reason, globalisation implies a modification of the reality of crime or, at least, the perception of crime;[88] that is, crimes that were previously of local importance have become problems of global guardianship,[89] such as economic crime.

Thus, the criminal law of globalisation faces 'a business delinquency of an economic nature, characterised by its organisational, professional, technical, complex and transnational component',[90] to which classical or traditional criminal law proves incapable of confronting. In this way, 'massive violations of human rights by multinational companies cannot and should not remain unanswered',[91] and there must be serious reflection 'about the appropriate legal instruments [. . .] to prevent and punish the terrible consequences they cause'.[92]

Thus, in the context of a globalised economy, supported by the emergence of a global society, we have witnessed the rise of a new perspective of Criminal Law to meet the expectations of this new social model[93]—that is, to encompass the protection of new interests and new criminal-legal goods. In other words, 'economic globalisation has forced criminal policy to face new challenges',[94] highlighting the

---

[85] Saad-Diniz (2018), p. 175.

[86] For more details: Masi and Moraes (2015), p. 18:16–43.

[87] Zaffaroni presents the main characteristics of this new moment, such as, for example, the technological revolution, the reduction of the economic regulatory power of the States and the concentration of capital. Zaffaroni (1999–2000), p: 71–96, pp. 74–75.

[88] Piedade ASC (2013), p. 97.

[89] 'In relation to the issue of global crime, it can be argued that not only are there new forms of transnational crime, but above all a new global perception of crime, which implies that certain local events acquire global resonance'. Vogel (2005). In: Cancio Meliá M (ed), p. 126.

[90] Sánchez (2019), p. 68.

[91] Crespo ED (2018), p. 23.

[92] Crespo ED (2018), p. 23.

[93] It is inseparable from the analysis of the new perspectives of Criminal Law the investigation of the social model in which it is found, since this reflects in that, as mentioned by Pierpaolo Bottini: 'The model of social organisation, structured on a model of economic production and on cultural and political values, establishes the mechanisms of power exercise with the aim of maintaining its functionality. The instruments of social control developed in various spheres of public and private relationships reflect the mentioned model [. . .]. *Criminal law and its institutes are characterised as mechanisms of social control and, therefore, receive the values and fulfil the objectives of the social model in which they are inserted* [. . .]'. (Our translation). Bottini PC (2010), p. 30. (our emphasis).

[94] Terradillos Basoco (2015), p. 9(35):7–36.

need for 'an ideal regulatory system to provide new and effective responses to new criminal phenomena'.[95]

Thus, an expansion of the criminal branch was observed with the aim of building new interests (or new valuations of pre-existing interests) that became apparent, notably with the effective emergence of poignant risks arising from technical progress, which fostered not only the development of new forms of crime but also contributed to the 'institutionalisation of insecurity'. This situation is felt by a society of fear,[96] whose most significant trait is the general feeling of insecurity, as an especially acute expression of living (in) risks.[97]

Increasingly, insecurity becomes a social claim to which it is assumed that the State and, especially, Criminal Law, should offer the appropriate response, eliciting, with greater clarity, an expansion of protection that puts an end to the anguish derived from uncertainties, such as the cases, for example, of demands in economic-business matters.[98] For this reason, indeed, we talk about economic delinquency and the company as delinquency 'of risks'.[99]

The economically globalised society is, then, a society of risks,[100] from which emerge political-criminal challenges to use criminal law as a tool for confronting (or managing)[101] the dangers arising from this new social framework. Legislative and dogmatic changes are observable in this context,[102] as well as modern criminological incursions (*v. infra*) to adapt the punitive structures.

Indeed, the general trend of creating new 'criminal-legal goods', with the expansion of legally and criminally relevant risk areas and, furthermore, with some

---

[95] Terradillos Basoco (2015), p. 13.

[96] Piedade ASC (2013), p. 97.

[97] Silva Sánchez (2013), pp. 38–40.

[98] Silva Sánchez (2013), p. 50–51. In the words of Eugenio Zaffaroni, 'Beyond the already classic attempt to contain the abuse of state power, criminologists, in recent years, 'have drawn attention to the real damage produced by other powers—especially the economic and financial ones—and want to go beyond criminology itself: *'Taking harm seriously'*. Zaffaroni (2015), p. 13.

[99] Lascuraín (2018) In: Mata Barranco NJ, Dopico Gómez-Aller J, Sánchez L, Nieto Martín A (eds), p. 37.

[100] Social model developed by the sociologist Ulrich Beck in his work 'Risk Society' and in his subsequent studies such as 'World Risk Society'.

[101] '[...] the use of criminal law as a mechanism for reinforcement and implementation of precautionary norms, the transformation of criminal law into a subsidiary norm of the rules of restriction or prohibition of activities over which there is uncertainty about the potential risks they offer. Criminal law, gradually, incorporates precaution as a guiding principle of certain criminal laws, to strengthen the risk management system, and to respond to social demands for greater control and for greater security'. (Our translation). Bottini PC (2010), p. 85.

[102] 'In this context, criminal law begins to guide its institutions towards prevention, to the inhibition of activities, at the moment preceding the causation of harm, before the affectation of the legally protected good. The criminal norm seeks to repress potentially harmful behaviours. The disvalue of the result is replaced by the disvalue of the action, the concrete damage is replaced by the probability of affecting goods and interests. Criminal types no longer harbour injury in their wording and direct their elements to danger, to risk'. (Our translation). Bottini PC (2010), p. 88.

flexibility in the rules of imputation and relativisation of the political-criminal principles of guarantee, refers to what has been designated as the 'expansion' of criminal law.[103]

Furthermore, the expansionist perspectives of the criminal branch bring paradigmatic changes to its entire configuration, which is why it is argued that we are facing a new face: a 'new' criminal law or, even, a 'modern' criminal law.[104]

The question behind this statement arises from the observation that, within the contours of contemporaneity, the classic, 'minimal', 'nuclear' criminal law, of liberal and guarantor matrix, focused on the protection of essentially personal and patrimonial goods,[105] no longer appears sufficiently capable of solving the modern problems of supra-individual criminality, necessitating 'structural modifications to adapt the repressive system to the phenomenon of risk society'.[106]

For this purpose, countless theoretical contributions are presented regarding the establishment of this new moment of Penal Science,[107] with dogmatic foundations to support the 'modernisation' of Criminal Law, based on the importance assumed by danger in the so-called Supra-individual Criminal Law, in which Economic Criminal Law is included.[108] In any case, this modern Criminal Law is a product of solid material and legal necessity that criminalists must assume and critically construct,[109] one of the most important tasks of criminal dogmatics being the adaptation of classic institutions to obtain useful tools for the protection of new legal goods arising from this new socio-economic development.[110]

In this scenario that depicts the current reality, the protection of legal goods in the economic sphere proves to be one of the fundamental challenges of the criminal (economic) branch, given not only the collective nature of the goods in question but

---

[103] Silva Sánchez (2013), p. 28.

[104] Arroyo Zapatero (2012) Política criminal y estado de derecho en las sociedades contemporáneas. In: Arroyo Zapatero L et al. (eds) *Derecho penal de la empresa: Del derecho penal económico del estado social al derecho penal de la empresa globalizado*. Ediar, Buenos Aires, p. 29.

[105] Arroyo Zapatero (2012), p. 177.

[106] Bottini PC (2010), p. 93.

[107] Evidently, the current scenario does not only bring theoretical contributions to justify the 'expansion' of criminal law, but also antagonistic outlines pointing to its possible illegitimacy: '*The question is ultimately raised from issues of legitimacy of criminal intervention in the protection of the so-called 'new risks'. Essentially, even though intermediate positions have also emerged, these antagonistic postures are concretised, on the one hand, in the theses of those who defend the legitimacy of criminal intervention only to the extent that it is confined to the proper scope of a minimal criminal law reduced to traditional or classic criminal law, to a nuclear criminal law—Kernstrafrecht—. On the reverse are the theses that accept the legitimacy of criminal intervention in new areas of social activity, in sectors where the supra-individual, collective, is in the foreground, accepting the legitimacy of the so-called accessory criminal law (Nebenstrafrecht) postulated in favour of guarantee theses* [. . .]'. (Our translation). Bidasolo (2008) ¿Cabe limitar la expansión del derecho penal pese a proteger nuevas modalidades delictivas? In: Zaffaroni ER, p. 151.

[108] Silveira (2012). *Boletim IBCCRIM* 20(238):6.

[109] Arroyo Zapatero (2012), p. 31.

[110] Lascano (2012). In: Arroyo Zapatero L et al. (eds), p. 46.

also the difficulties of typifying the offence and the frequent use of abstract danger crimes.[111] Indeed, as Anabela Miranda Rodrigues points out, the risks in the economic sphere are not mere illusory events,[112] being, in truth, aggressions to legal goods in 'contexts of collective action', where personal relations are replaced by 'anonymous and standardised behaviours', widened by greater insecurity in the face of the 'neutrality' or the 'external appearance of legality' of economic crimes, 'which frustrate the identification of victims as such'.[113]

For Terradillos Basoco,[114] it is no longer possible to continue ignoring the presence of major economic delinquency, often transnational and organised, according to the parameters of the company, necessitating the direction of criminal policy to confront this type of criminality, which has the legal person as the central framework of economic criminal phenomena.

This specific business framework focuses not only on the relevant interests and strategies of criminal policy but also on the dogmatic scenario, in order to reveal, among other aspects: (i) the delimitation of the affected legal goods, with due attention to the principles of harmfulness and legality; (ii) the quantitative and qualitative plurality of regulatory sources, which obliges criminal norms to integrate with other normative levels; (iii) the perspective of plurality and heterogeneity of subjects in the business structure; and (iv) the need for the revision of the principle *societas delinquere non potest.*[115]

In this regard, the controversial aspect of economic criminal law is pointed out, which concerns how legitimate its intervention is, as well as the unlimited expansion of the *jus puniendi* in the field of safeguarding contemporary legal assets, notably in this case, the economic order—consisting of the essential characteristics of the economic model, linked to the production, circulation and distribution of wealth.[116] In this new field of challenges, it is necessary to 'implement responses consistent with the specific characteristics of the reality to be addressed, as ignorance or neglect lead to inefficiency'.[117]

From these outlines, it is understood that contemporary social problems, such as corruption, are directed towards criminal law as the primary source of protection.[118]

---

[111] Rodrigues (2019) *Direito penal económico: uma política criminal na era do compliance* (Manuais universitários). Almedina, Coimbra, p. 26.

[112] '*It cannot be otherwise when traditional crime accounts for 94% of known crimes, but the remaining 6% represents 65% of the damage caused by criminal behaviour*'. Terradillos Basoco (2012) In: Arroyo Zapatero L et al. (eds), p. 97.

[113] Rodrigues (2019), p. 26.

[114] Terradillos Basoco (2012), pp. 97–99.

[115] Terradillos Basoco (2012), pp. 99–100.

[116] Bercovici and Souza (2013). In: Oliveira WT et al. (eds), p. 24.

[117] Rodrigues (2019), p. 28.

[118] The question raised by Zaffaroni is immediately posed: '[. . .] we are not unaware that the repression of crimes against humanity imposes a similar problem on criminal law: the worst thing that can happen is that it extends the naive conviction that the punishment of genocides prevents the production of new genocides'. (Our translation). Zaffaroni (2015), p. 14.

The issue, however, deserves better scrutiny in understanding that this protection cannot be the exclusive function of criminal law, and also of economic criminal law—a fact that 'would ultimately reveal a (problem of) lack of legitimacy of criminal intervention in this domain'.[119]

On the other hand, it is not about inhibiting or resisting the criminalisation of irregular economic activities, especially when they affect essential legal assets. 'Between excess and abstention from punishment, between fleeing to criminal law and fleeing from criminal law [...] is the balance between the demands for protection of new legal assets and the use of criminal law as the last resort of criminal policy'.[120]

As Eugenio Zaffaroni suggests,[121] there is a need for a 'prudent criminal approach' or even 'criminal prudence' regarding the application of criminal law in the economic field, in order to reflect on the performance of criminal frameworks within the new protection network and seek appropriate solutions to the general theory, 'without prejudice to the general warning about the need for effective prevention in another field of law'.[122]

For this reason, a new context of prevention of corporate crime has influenced different legal forms to confront this reality. The 'culture of compliance' has been silently decreeing the loss of state functions—notably, in this case, of Criminal Law—in addressing economic crimes, giving rise to a global movement of 'self-constitutionalisation' promoted by corporate codes of conduct.[123]

In this sense, criminal intervention in the economic field, as a 'legal Darwinism',[124] has been adapting to the challenges that are posed to it, notably to debates about (il)legitimacy and the deficit of punishability, with the so-called criminal compliance as a new tool.[125]

Criminal (economic) law in the era of compliance operates as a stimulus for the company to avoid committing illegal acts, within a prevention strategy that repositions Criminal Law to its ideal role as a last resort, in a variation of the concept of traditional (formal) social control attributed to Criminal Law.[126]

---

[119] Later, the author mentions: 'What is at stake is to ensure the legitimacy of penal intervention in economic activity that resolves, through an appropriate balance of values, the tensions between the demands for protection of collective legal goods, increasingly "immaterial" or "institutionalised," and respect for the principle of the *ultima ratio* in which that penal intervention is embodied. In fact, the limits to the *jus puniendi* must coexist with the state's obligation to ensure preventive needs'. Rodrigues (2019), pp. 27–28.

[120] Rodrigues (2019), pp. 27–28.

[121] Zaffaroni (2015), p. 20.

[122] Zaffaroni (2015), p. 20. Continuing, he points out: 'It seems obvious to us that the law must prepare a legal effort of preventive control that cannot be limited to national law, but rather must —sooner or later—advance in the field of international law. Criminal law should blush at this effort, but in no way exhaust it and, even less, create the illusion that it does'. (Our translation). Zaffaroni (2015), p. 20.

[123] Saad-Diniz (2014), p. 113.

[124] Arroyo Zapateroand Nieto Martín (eds) (2013), p. 11.

[125] Silveira and Saad-Diniz(2015), p. 66 and 71.

[126] Silveira and Saad-Diniz (2015), p. 124.

3.2 Economic Criminology: The Criminological Experience as a Reflective Vector for Preventive Measures and the Delimitation of Criminal Responsibility

The incursions of this work are inevitably intertwined with the criminality produced by companies or through them, so that, whatever the methodological-dogmatic approach given to the topic, the inseparable link between the protection of human rights and business activity will persist.

Presenting the criminological contributions of economic crime will contribute not only to the evaluation of the compliance tool, especially with regard to 'effectiveness metrics'[127]—as will be seen in the next section—but also, and especially, to verify the corporate victimisation process, particularly when proposing to analyse possible prevention of human rights violations resulting from business activity.

The essentiality of bringing contributions from Criminology to the discussion is initially established by the validity of its empirical and interdisciplinary scientific method of analysing and observing the criminal phenomenon, not only shedding light on the study of the crime and the criminal but also being concerned with the victim and with the mechanisms of social control,[128] therefore fundamental to the proposed study of this work.

Furthermore, Criminology, by reaching a scope of intervention that Criminal Law is not capable of achieving on its own, proves capable of providing valid information not only about the genesis and dynamics of crime but also about pre and post-criminal issues, so as to provide effective prevention strategies.[129] This means that by understanding the theories developed about corporate criminal behaviour, we gain a better understanding of the phenomenon in order to explore more effectively possible preventive parameters.

Thus, in the pursuit of analysing the established hypotheses, combining their main arcs, the adoption of an interdisciplinary perspective is necessary, whether to discuss the legitimacy of the 'new' Criminal Law to regulate new areas demanding protection (such as those regulated by Economic Criminal Law, notably in the fight against corruption), or to analyse, from a criminological perspective, the development of theories explaining criminal deviation in the corporate context, notably to reflect—subsequently—on the deterrent strategies for this phenomenon.[130]

Therefore, the perspectives of Criminology are adopted as a reflective vector capable of guiding the critical analysis of *compliance* programmes, especially when little has been envisaged regarding the scientific scrutiny of their evaluation, given that, in most cases, such instruments 'end up being confused with other

[127] Saad-Diniz (2018), p. 167.

[128] Shecaira (2020), p. 51.

[129] Francia (2018) In: Crespo E, Nieto Martín A (eds), pp. 194–195.

[130] Souza (2021), p. 22.

company controls, reduced to a "façade," or, what is even worse, to the appearance of "an ethical renewal"'.[131]

In this sense, criminological research can contribute to criminal-political action, pointing out recommendations for regulatory policies, strategies of *enforcement* and concrete actions of corporate self-regulation, particularly from the verification of the 'real needs of *compliance,* what the profile of the offenders is, who and how is victimised, what the dimensions of the damage caused by the socially harmful behaviour are'.[132]

In this sense, given the clear negative effects arising from processes of corporate victimisation (that is, serious violations of human rights) and, above all, in the face of the current variety of corporate scandals, it is pertinent, if not fundamental, to bring to the research references 'more substantial for a redefinition of how corporate offences are conceived, the levels of damage caused to the victim and the contexts in which corporate offences occur'.[133]

Furthermore, in addition to this reflective vector contributing to the criminological review of the prevention of corporate offences,[134] it allows, through its lines, the verification of alternatives to the attribution of responsibility to companies, investigating the pertinence, or lack thereof, of the adoption of the CLLE.

3.2.1 Criminological Aspects of the Formulation of the Aetiology of Corporate Crime

Despite criminological thought having been dedicated for some time to understanding the aspects related to economically natured offences, only recently has Criminology begun to inquire, in a systematic way, about the aetiology of the criminal phenomenon in the corporate context,[135] adopting, for this purpose, a new criminological perspective, in which the focus is not the mere sum of the conduct of individuals (economic agents), but rather the behaviour of the corporation itself.[136]

However, before we elevate this new approach, it is essential to understand the evolution of criminological thought in the economic field in order to have sufficient foundations to understand the deviation of an economic-criminal nature in the context of complex organisations, especially the relationship between white-

[131] Saad-Diniz (2018), p. 168.

[132] Saad-Diniz (2018), p 169.

[133] Saad-Diniz (2019),p. 144.

[134] Saad-Diniz (2018), p. 168.

[135] '*Explanations of criminal behaviour historically have focused on the behaviour of individuals. The criminality of organisations, or corporate criminology, has only recently received systematic attention from researchers and policy makers*'. (Our translation). Albanese (1984), p. 11.

[136] Souza and Coelho (2021). In: Choukr FH, Japiassú CEA (eds), p. 17.

collar crime, occupational crime and corporate crime.[137] Broadly speaking, while *white-collar crime* refers to an offence committed by a person of high reputation within the framework of their professional activity, occupational crime is one where the social position of the offender is not decisive, but rather the fact that the criminal deviation occurred during a certain activity. Finally, *corporate crime* emphasises the fact that the offence occurred within a business organisation.[138]

Regarding this last aetiology, it is understood that the company is the centre capable of generating or favouring the practice of criminally illicit acts, that is, the company has become a centre around which different illicit activities can be conceived.[139]

If criminology has always been dedicated to the classic crimes and criminals of the Enlightenment, particularly street crime, with the social transformations of the last century, especially globalisation, this scientific field has had its study area altered by the effects of economic crime, forcing criminological science to seek the hitherto ignored approaches of criminals holding power and speculative capital.[140]

It was especially through the legacy of Edwin Hardin Sutherland and his theory of differential association that new actors and new criminal figures were included in criminological research. This is because, if before, crime and the criminal were seen from merely biological perspectives (pathologies) or sociopathological ones (poverty, unemployment, living in ghettos, etc.),[141] from the author's ideas, it was highlighted that the 'social position and the *status* of individuals is not only relevant but is essential to understand the cause of crime'.[142]

The turning point of criminology occurred with the famous speech by Sutherland, delivered to the *American Sociological Society* in December 1939, innovatively titled *White-Collar Criminality*.[143] The title announces, from the outset, that the study proposes to combine crime with economic activities, to highlight the notable occurrence of crime in the upper class or white-collar sector, and to refute the classic theories of the time that associated the criminal phenomenon with poverty—that is, with the lower classes of society.

---

[137] Souza and, Coelho (2021).

[138] Nieto Martín (2019) In: Saad-Diniz E, Gomes R (eds), p. 63.

[139] Souza and Japiassú (2017), p. 1031–1051. The authors, citing José Faria Costa, note that one can 'outline various types of economic criminality: (a) a criminality that develops on the margins of the company, thus not touching the company itself; (b) the criminality that germinates within the company against the company itself; (c) the criminality carried out by people from the company against other members of the company, and, finally, (d) the criminality that projects from the company'. Saad-Diniz (2019).

[140] Souza (2011), p 107.

[141] Souza (2011), p 110.

[142] Saad-Diniz (2019), p. 61.

[143] Sutherland (2014), pp. 93–103.

From the author's perspective, the general theories of criminal behaviour that justified poverty as the cause of crime were based on biased evidence of reality,[144] since these only presented the spectrum of crimes that reached the criminal justice agencies of the time and excluded 'vast areas of criminal behaviour of people who do not belong to the lower class'.[145]

Thus, Sutherland sought to develop a theory that would serve to explain not only the criminality of the lower class but also 'all modalities of crimes and all modalities of criminals',[146] especially the criminality coming from the 'business world', since 'the financial cost of white collar crime is probably much higher than those crimes traditionally considered as "criminal problem"' and, moreover, 'reduces social morale and produces large-scale social disorganisation'.[147]

He thus proposed the theory of differential association as a general explanatory cause of criminality, presenting the idea that any systematic criminality is 'learned in direct or indirect association with those who already practice the behaviour' and 'those who learn this criminal behaviour are separated from intimate and frequent contacts with law-abiding behaviour'.[148]

Thus, criminal behaviour would develop within a social group (lower or upper class) and would be derived from frequent and intimate interaction with individuals who violate certain norms. In this context, definitions favourable to the transgression of the law outweigh definitions favourable to the obedience of the law.[149] Therefore, there would be a differential organisation of learning criminal values in the sense that 'man learns deviant behaviour and associates himself with it'.[150]

Putting his theory to empirical test, Sutherland investigated judicial decisions and administrative commission rulings against seventy of the largest commercial and industrial corporations in North America, concluding, notably, that *white-collar crime is a crime*, or, in other words, that white-collar crime was indeed and definitively a reality.[151] However, he found that such crime did not carry the

[144] 'The theory that criminal behaviour in general is due to poverty or the psychopathic and sociopathic conditions associated with it, can be considered invalid for three reasons. Firstly, the generalisation is based on a biased sample that almost completely omits the behaviour of white-collar criminals. Criminologists have restricted their database, more for reasons of convenience and ignorance than principle, most of the time, to cases from criminal courts and juvenile courts, and these agencies are mainly used for criminals from lower economic strata. Consequently, their databases are grossly biased from the point of view of the economic status of the criminals and the generalisation that criminality is linked with poverty is not justified'. Sutherland (2014), p. 101.

[145] Sutherland (2014), p. 94.

[146] Souza (2011), p. 110.

[147] Sutherland (2014), p. 97.

[148] Sutherland (2014), p. 102.

[149] Souza (2011), p. 111.

[150] Shecaira (2020), p. 226.

[151] Sutherland (1999) *White-collar crime*. La Piqueta, Madrid, p. 73.

same criminal stigma as the offences hitherto of concern to criminology; that is, the economic criminal did not carry the same popular stereotype of a delinquent.[152]

In other words, the problem with economic crime was that business practices such as unfair competition, misleading advertising, violations of labour rights, financial fraud/manipulation, patent infringement, among others,[153] were not seen as criminal and were treated differently by the penal system itself. Identifying this problem, 'Sutherland noted the absence of identity and perception of these practices as delinquency, in the legal, judicial, social and theoretical spheres'.[154] It became evident, from the criticisms he pointed out, that there existed 'gaps in repression that protect offensive economic activities, notwithstanding the potential social harm (disvalue of the result) and disvalue of the action'.[155]

In trying to understand why there is a different treatment between offenders from different social strata, Sutherland developed his general theory based on a new criminological aetiology.[156] When initiating specific studies of the theory of the white-collar criminal, he sought a definition of delinquency perpetrated by high-level businesspeople[157] 'against one or more of the following classes of victims: consumers, competitors, shareholders, inventors and employees, as well as against the State in the form of tax fraud and bribery of public officials'.[158]

In this way, assuming the general aetiology of the theory of differential association, oriented towards the learning of deviant behaviour,[159] Sutherland proposes the

[152] '*When the stigma of crime is imposed as a punishment, the accused is placed within the popular stereotype of "the criminal."* [...] *in modern society the stereotype is largely limited to the lower socioeconomic class.* [...] *the procedures of criminal law are modified so that the stigma of crime does not connect with the offenders. [...] these crimes generally have not been included within the field of criminology*'. Sutherland (1999), p. 99–100.

[153] Sutherland presents statistics of a series of business criminal practices through specific chapters in: Sutherland (1999).

[154] Costa (2011), p. 71.

[155] Neves (2011), p. 65.

[156] '[...] *the crime of "white collar" has its genesis in the same general process as other criminal behaviour, namely, differential association. The hypothesis of differential association suggests that criminal behaviour is learned in association with those who define that behaviour favourably and in isolation from those who define it unfavourably; and that a person in an appropriate situation participates in this criminal behaviour when, or only when, the weight of favourable definitions outweighs that of unfavourable definitions. This hypothesis is certainly not a complete or universal explanation of "white collar" crime or any other crime, but it may perhaps agree with the data of both types of crime, better than any other general hypothesis*'. Sutherland (1999), p. 277.

[157] Souza (2011), p. 113.

[158] Sutherland (1999), p. 261.

[159] 'Sutherland started from the differentiation between conventional deviant behaviour and occupational, seeking to explain the fact that this latter criminality comes, curiously, accompanied by predominant respect for the legal order and social rules. It is only due to the structures of opportunity and learning within organisations that individuals find the necessary conditions to engage in economic criminality—and this, also curiously, without the same individual ceasing to morally condemn those who commit a traditional crime'. (Our translation). Saad-Diniz (2018), p. 171.

concept of *white-collar crime* as the 'offence committed by a person of high respectability and *status* social in the course of his occupation'.[160] Thus, 'the offenders belonging to that category are people from the upper social strata who, like any others, violate criminal laws due to a process of learning in their respective social segment (economic activity)'.[161]

Although there is no room in this work for further deepening, there is no doubt about the theoretical influence that Edwin H. Sutherland provided for the consolidation of economic criminology,[162] drawing public, legal and academic attention to the forms of behaviour of powerful people that destroy the integrity of society.[163] His importance endures to the present day, especially due to the 'ideological bias'[164] detected by him more than half a century ago.

In other words, even in current times, the reality remains vivid in which the white-collar criminal is not detectable within the delinquent stereotype, is not seen as deserving of criminal reproach, there being, in practical terms, 'a persistent maintenance, within the formal control agencies—police, justice and prison—, of a *preferential option* for the lower social strata',[165] in a scenario quite comparable to that presented by Sutherland.

Indeed, Eduardo Saad-Diniz[166] warns about the need—when dealing with the topic of economic and corporate crime—to make new efforts that allow for redefining the moral justifications that impose on the criminal justice system[167] 'an obsessive punishment, with intolerable levels of selectivity, stigmatisation and mass incarceration', notably due to the moral priority given to street crime. In his words, it is necessary, on the contrary, 'to account for the protagonism of corporations in socially harmful behaviour'.[168]

---

[160] These violations of the law by people of high socioeconomic class are conveniently called 'white-collar' crimes. [...] The 'white collar' crime can be defined, approximately, as a crime committed by a person of high respectability and *status* in the course of their occupation. Consequently, many high social class crimes are excluded, such as most cases of murder, adultery, intoxication, etc., as these are not generally part of their occupational procedures. Also excluded are abuses of trust by wealthy underworld members, as they are not people of respectability and high *status* social. Sutherland (1999), p. 65.

[161] Souza (2011), p. 114.

[162] Saad-Diniz (2011), p. 63.

[163] Geis (2011), p. 3.

[164] Expression coined by: Souza (2011), p. 117.

[165] Souza (2011), p. 114.

[166] Saad-Diniz (2019), p. 14.

[167] For Zaffaroni and Pierangeli, the penal system is the institutionalised punitive social control that, in practice, encompasses the moment when a suspicion of a crime is detected or presumed to be detected until a penalty is imposed and executed, presupposing a normative activity that creates the law that institutionalises the procedure, the performance of officials and the definition of cases and conditions for this performance. This is the general idea of the 'penal system' in a limited sense, encompassing the activity of the legislator, the public, the police, the judges, the prosecutors and the penal execution officials. Zaffaroni and Pierangeli (2001), p. 70.

[168] Zaffaroni and Pierangeli (2001).

The author adds: 'It is necessary to deepen Sutherland's legacy on crime occurring in the corporate environment and intensify it in relation to crime committed *by* the corporations themselves [. . .]'.[169] It is no coincidence that this work notes Sutherland's conceptions as a starting point to analyse the criminological implications of the business-economic scenario, notably to account—in the next topic—for the convergences that corporate criminology has in relation to the resulting victimological process, that is, the damages caused by white-collar crime.

Furthermore, up to now, it is understood that Sutherland's theory of differential association, presupposed from a learning process likely to occur in the upper classes (*white-collar*), has a prominent relationship with business crime, as the theory focuses on the interior of the corporation and the importance that the collective environment has for the occurrence of delinquency.[170] It is certain that the 'reason why some organisations violate laws, while others do not, is the process of differential association'.[171] Some even say that corporate crime is fundamentally white-collar crime.[172]

Even after Sutherland admitted that his theory was not a comprehensive explanation of corporate crime, it remained the only one subsequently used to explain the involvement of companies in a series of crimes. Only in the 1970s, after the Watergate scandal, did new theoretical strands emerge to advance criminological thinking about the corporation.[173]

In any case, advancing in the criminological thinking of the corporation, attempts to explain business crime ended up introducing into the investigation of crime and the criminal justice system constructions of the type 'corporate entity' (*corporate entity*) and 'corporate action' (*corporate action*), covering simultaneously all types of crime and offenders.[174] As Nieto Martín points out, after Sutherland's legacy, the common denominator of theories after the 1970s was to

---

[169] Zaffaroni and Pierangeli (2001), p. 15.

[170] La conducta desviada es fruto del aprendizaje. Se aprende cuando una persona se asocia con aquéllos que defienden la conveniencia de este tipo de comportamientos y se aleja de aquellos otros que lo consideran como algo perjudicial. Cuando los argumentos favorables a la comisión del delito acaban pesando sobre los desfavorables aparece el comportamiento delictivo. *Las personas que se integran en una organización aprenden cómo cometer determinadas infracciones y cómo justificarlas*. Por esta razón dejan de lado sus valores previos, de acuerdo con los cuales era impensable realizar determinados comportamientos' (our emphasis). NIETO MARTÍN, Adán. Introduction to Economic and Corporate Criminal Law. *In*: Economic and Corporate Criminal Law. NIETO MARTÍN *et al.* Madrid: Editorial Dykinson, 2018. *E-book*, p. 42.

[171] ALBANESE, Jay. S. Corporate criminology: Explaining deviance of business and political organisations. *Journal of Criminal Justice*, New York, v. 12, p. 11–19, 1984, p. 12.

[172] Saad-Diniz (2018), p. 173.

[173] 'New efforts to explain corporate criminality did not emerge until the 1970s, sparked largely by the Watergate scandal and the subsequent disclosures of domestic and foreign payments by American corporations. A recent review discovered only six additional attempts to systematically explain corporate criminality since Sutherland's pioneering work during the 1940s'. Albanese (1984), p. 12.

[174] Saad-Diniz (2019), p. 65.

highlight the idea that the corporation is the main cause of delinquent conduct, leaving individual or social factors of the offending individual in the background. The paradigm became, therefore, the structural idea of *corporate crime*.[175]

To explain more specifically the theory of *corporate crime* as a structural offence, the Spanish author highlights that stating that delinquent conducts committed in a corporation are structural offences means saying that their criminological explanation is established by 'environmental factors, coming from the group, and that, additionally, the power structure within the company is what determines the people with a higher "penal risk," through the construction, for example, of scapegoats'.[176]

Following, in many ways, the lines of the theory of differential association, the structural theory presented by Nieto Martín brings new perspectives to the conception that deviant conduct is learned by associating with those favourable to criminal behaviour, overcoming any unfavourable arguments; that is, 'contact with the group's values would give them the necessary reasons to set aside their moral scruples and commit the crime'.[177] The conclusion is drawn that both external and internal factors are decisive in the formation of the 'criminal spirit of the group'.[178]

Going further in the field of explanatory theories of corporate crime, the neutralisation theory presented by Gresham M. Skeys and David Matza suggests that criminal conduct occurs because offenders find reasons to justify (neutralise) the guilt arising from the violation of the law (*justifications of deviant behaviour*),[179] thereby overcoming moral or cultural barriers that could prevent the commission of the offence.[180] In the authors' view, neutralisation techniques would correspond to the 'definitions favourable to the violation of the law' pointed out by Sutherland.[181]

Skyes and Matza present five main neutralisation techniques: (i) denial of responsibility; (ii) denial of the harm done; (iii) denial of the victim; (iv) 'condemnation of the condemners'; and (v) appeal to higher loyalty.[182] Because these

---

[175] Nieto Martín (2019), pp. 62–63.

[176] Nieto Martín (2019), p. 63.

[177] Nieto Martín (2019), p. 64.

[178] The group's criminal spirit would be a code of values deviated from corporate culture, in the author's words 'a set of technical attitudes of committing criminal acts, of arguments and rationalisation [. . .]'. Nieto Martín (2019), p. 65.

[179] Sykes and Matza (1957), p. 664.

[180] Nieto Martín (2018), p. 42.

[181] Sykes and Matza (1957), p. 667.

[182] Discussing the techniques, Gueiros and Coelho state that: 'In the case of corporate crimes, the main techniques would be (1) denial of responsibility ("I was forced to do it, because it was an order within the company," "it was common practice there"), (2) attributing the damage to the victim's own conduct ("workplace accidents occur in most cases due to the worker's recklessness"), (3) the convenience or rationality of evading the law ("the tax pressure was excessive and did not allow us to compete") and (4) the appeal to higher loyalties ("I had to increase the company's sales and, in this way, guarantee the employment of many people")'. (Our translation). Souza and Coelho (2021), p. 19.

techniques place high importance on the organisation (or group), Nieto Martin, in pointing out that the key issue is determining how a deviant culture arises within a company, indicates the essentiality of leadership in establishing ethics in the corporate environment.[183]

Another approach contributing to the analysis of *corporate crime* is the opportunity theory, which presents the idea that a series of routine activities increases the likelihood of deviant offences, converging on three elements: (a) motivated offenders, (b) suitable objects and victims and (c) the absence of effective protectors. Within this scheme, crime is more related to its form of occurrence than to why or by whom.[184]

There are also the 'strain theories' or 'anomie theory', by which the criminal behaviour of certain individuals would occur because they are unable to achieve certain goals (social, professional gratifications or avoidance of negative situations); they would channel their frustration into committing the offence as an easier means to achieve the planned ends.[185]

According to the Spanish author, this situation routinely presents itself in our capitalist model, as it is immersed in a situation of 'practically structural tension', in which, within an organisation, problems and risks are passed from the top to the weakest links (*risk slippage*),[186] favouring the practice of illicit acts in order to achieve the intended business results.[187]

The other criminological approach on which economic criminality is based is the rational choice theory (*rational choice theory*) proposed by Gary Stanley Becker, of a markedly utilitarian current.[188] Revitalising the ideas of the Classical School (e.g., Beccaria and Betham), this theory asserts that 'economic offenders result from the paradigm of the calculating offender, whose decision to offend is preceded by a cold weighing of the disadvantages and advantages that the criminal conduct can bring them'.[189]

---

[183] Nieto Martín (2018), p. 43.

[184] Nieto Martín (2019), p. 71.

[185] The author exemplifies: 'la aparición de mayor competencia puede llevar a que empresas que antes actuaban prácticamente en un régimen de monopolio adopten prácticas ilícitas como la corrupción para conseguir mantener su cuota de mercado'. Nieto Martín (2018), p. 43.

[186] Nieto Martín (2018), p. 43.

[187] 'The pressure that is exerted on the company's senior leadership quickly moves to the weakest links. The leaders of a Companies operating in a competitive environment and needing to secure new projects will demand sales from their salespeople at any cost, even if that cost involves obtaining contracts, for example, through bribery or anti-competitive agreements. This shift of risk and responsibility, from senior leaders to middle management, is one of the most distinctive features of any organisation and also serves to explain the etiology of criminal behaviour'. (Our translation). Ibid, p. 44.

[188] One could speak of 'maximum utility for the offender'. Nieto Martín (2019), p. 68.

[189] Nieto Martín (2019), p. 63.

In other words, it is argued that delinquent behaviour stems from rationality, so that, in an economic analysis (*economic approach*),[190] both individuals and legal entities would commit offences due to the financial return or other rewards derived from the crime.[191] In this way, 'the perpetrator of economic crimes would be a rational actor who weighs the costs and benefits derived from criminal behaviour'.[192]

Nieto Martín asserts that there is a certain consensus that the theory of rational choice would have a high explanatory yield in economic delinquency, as corporations, like individuals, are in a better position to assess costs and benefits compared to the delinquents of the Classical Era. This is because 'the existence of a business organisation allows for more efficient decision-making and information processing',[193] not to mention that, within a group, an individual's attitude towards risk becomes more prone to criminality, since 'if the delinquent conduct is assumed jointly, it is easier for a choice favourable to the commission of the offence to arise'.[194]

Although many authors admit the benefits of readings based on the utility and personal characteristics of managers and employees of business organisations, they point out, on the other hand, that such analyses only partially address the problem of economic crime.[195] For this reason, Saad-Diniz advises the need to critically consider traditional interpretations of the motivation for such crime, especially as a way to 'overcome reductionist readings of cost and benefit and ideations about the excessive ambition of managers'.[196]

It is necessary to bear in mind, as Saad-Diniz points out, the need to open scientific research to the field of economic criminology based on more consistent data collection and the maturation of scientific evidence. This is because, since the foundations of post-classical criminology, the collection of 'empirical data consolidated in the analysis of scientific evidence is the unequivocal path for the formulation of political-criminal action strategies'.[197]

This means that empirical analysis of the evidence is fundamental to determine, for example, 'what the profile of the offenders is, who and how they are victimised, what the dimensions of the damage caused by socially harmful corporate behaviour are, what the preferred alternatives for restoration would be'.[198]

It is worth mentioning, at this point, the usefulness of criminology in the development of public policies that allow for understanding, within the corporate vision, the introduction of criminal liability for corporations and the growing

---

[190] Becker (1968), p. 169–217. Available at: https://doi.org/10.1086/259394.

[191] Souza and Coelho (2021), p. 27.

[192] Nieto Martín (2018), p. 44.

[193] Nieto Martín (2019), p. 68.

[194] Nieto Martín (2019), p. 68.

[195] Souza and Coelho (2021), p. 19.

[196] Saad-Diniz (2018), p. 172.

[197] Saad-Diniz (2018), pp. 168–169.

[198] Saad-Diniz (2018), p. 169.

importance of compliance programmes.[199] Nieto Martín explains, for example, that internal prevention and detection models are mechanisms to compensate for any criminogenic factors that may exist within the organisation. This is because the formation of ethical conduct codes constitutes a counterweight to neutralisation techniques (see above) or, furthermore, confronts the theory of opportunity, as it would reduce opportunities for bribery or internal information disclosure.[200]

Scientific evidence 'makes more solid recommendations on regulatory policies, enforcement strategies and concrete actions of corporate self-regulation'[201] possible, so as to present the 'relevance of scientific investigation into the causes, controls and regulation strategies', especially, on the one hand, in the 'individualisation of agents, dimensions of damage, victimisation processes, to what extent one can speak of a deterrent or preventive effect, evaluation of the quality of enforcement initiatives', and, on the other hand, as a way to overcome 'the repressive mentality and attachment to formal social control, discussing the possibilities of establishing collaborative links between private action and regulatory and supervisory bodies'.[202]

3.2.2 Aspects of Corporate Victimology and the Corporate Violation of Human Rights

When considering compliance tools as a possible mechanism for the protection of human rights and as mechanisms for preventing irregularities, it is relevant not only to focus on the analysis of criminal behaviour in corporate settings as a reflective way of analysing deterrent parameters, but also to seek foundations for understanding the victimological process resulting from socially harmful corporate behaviour.

If, on the one hand, Criminology is directed towards the study of criminal reality, providing empirical data to guide criminal policy, on the other hand, it also provides reference elements for crime prevention and the defence of human rights and victims.[203] In this latter aspect, it would be pertinent to overcome the traditional orientation towards the author and direct attention to the fact, the criminal act and the nature of the criminal offence, assuming an orientation driven by awareness of the damages caused—social, material and human.[204]

Thus, in a contemporary convergence between economic criminology and human rights, it is pertinent to assume the latter not only as a negative structure to punitive intervention but also to understand them as a positive foundation for protecting victims of crimes, especially when, at present, economic crimes derived

[199] Nieto Martín (2018), p. 45.
[200] Nieto Martín (2018), p. 45.
[201] Saad-Diniz (2018), p. 169.
[202] Nieto Martín (2018), pp. 173–174.
[203] Francia (2018), p. 195.
[204] Francia (2018), p. 197–198.

from the corporate sphere form complex victimisation processes, which directly affect a large number of people (and indirectly, entire communities) who often cannot even acknowledge their own victim status.[205]

To promote, albeit briefly, reflections from criminology and corporate victimology will allow us to identify to what extent criminal behaviour affects human rights, verifying the residue of corporate victimisation or the 'hidden figure' of corporate crime[206] in order to understand or glimpse the best way to combat it, prevent it and repair the damages caused by it.

In terms of this work, it is intended to investigate the performance of *compliance* instruments as possible mechanisms for preventing human rights violations in the corporate sphere. In this sense, it is insightful to present perspectives on the construction of corporate victim conflict as a way to contribute to the formulation of prevention strategies and the reduction of victimisation by these compliance programmes.

This becomes even more pertinent when we verify, from the ideas of William S. Laufer—a North American reference on the subject—that we still fail in the conceptions of corporate criminal responsibility. This is because accountability norms end up being replaced by a type of regulation that allows companies to opt out of the criminal justice system, enabling them to strategically reformulate their guilt and manage their reputation intelligently. The weakness with which Corporate Criminal Law emerges substantially undermines the potential for regulatory persuasion (*deterrence*), as for there to be cooperative models of regulation and criminal responsibility, criminal law must be the last resort. Thus, if there is an effective threat of criminal law, less formal social controls, such as self-regulation, would be leveraged.[207]

In addition to this, corporate victimology could provide more substantial elements for the proposal of forms of corporate criminal responsibility attribution, less obsessed with formal social control and more suitable to 'respond to questions of how to punish, what type of punishment, at what intensity, and what type of restoration to what type of victim should be considered'.[208]

It is essential to clarify, from the outset, that the concept of corporate victimology (*corporate victimology*) is presented as a new field in criminal sciences in Brazil by Professor Eduardo Saad-Diniz. For him, the efforts originating from this new theoretical body will contribute to evaluations about the possible links between the damages caused by corporations and criteria for attributing responsibility to corporations, in such a way as to abandon the emotional appeal of the

[205] Francia (2018), p. 203. Also, Saad-Diniz mentions: 'The difficulties in protecting victims involved in corporate scandals are enormous, and the void in terms of social control strategies and regulation is even greater. The social mobilisation against white-collar crime and the network of protection for corporate victims have not yet found concrete expression in society [...]'. (Our translation). Saad-Diniz (2019), p. 116.

[206] Laufer (2019), p. 8.

[207] Laufer (2006), pp. 5–6.

[208] Saad-Diniz (2019), p. 135.

criminal justice system for the incrimination of individuals—redefining, even, their moral justifications (*moral justifications*)—and to account for the protagonism of corporations in socially harmful behaviour.[209]

Furthermore, for Saad-Diniz,[210] this new scientific branch can enable evaluations regarding the possible links between the damages caused by corporations, the development of victimisation prevention policies and damage reduction, as well as provide conditions for the subsequent development of effectiveness evaluation indicators for victimisation prevention policies. With this, the strictly normative approach to research in the corporate sphere is overcome, which ends up mobilising prophylactic measures of low persuasive potential and prevention standards based on non-measurable 'effectiveness'.

In these terms, the development of corporate victimology proposed by Saad-Diniz—based on the review of traditional fields and highlighted through the reconstruction of criminological and victimological knowledge—aims to direct, in a critical manner, more sophisticated (and less obsessive) measures of formal social control, thus encompassing elementary notions of who is the victim of corporate crime, how she is affected and what reaction or preventive measure can be considered most appropriate to be adopted by the criminal justice system and the regulation of corporate abuse.[211]

Thus, summarising the propositions of William S. Laufer, the author notes that it is up to 'corporate victimology, as a new field of research for criminal sciences, to find the points of integration between offender and victim, to understand the causes of corporate violence, how to conceive it and how to measure it'.[212] This, moreover, reinforces 'the commitment of States to increase the strategies of social control of corporations to the same extent that it overcomes moral indifference to the processes of corporate victimisation'.[213]

In terms of the different categories and levels of victimisation,[214] we speak, in the present analysis, of victimisation caused *by* the company, in such a way as to highlight the category in which the causes and consequences of socially harmful corporate behaviour are evaluated, generating social contexts of direct and indirect victimisation, especially at the analytical level, in which the company offends individuals, communities, *stakeholders,* or the state itself.[215]

---

209 Saad-Diniz (2019), pp. 13–14.

210 Saad-Diniz (2019), pp. 13–14 and 110.

211 Saad-Diniz (2019), pp. 143–144.

212 Saad-Diniz (2019), p. 148.

213 Saad-Diniz (2019), p. 150.

214 'In addition to scale (large, medium and minor offensive potential) and the traditional categories of victimology (primary, secondary and tertiary), there are other levels of victimisation experience […]. Of particular interest for understanding socially harmful behaviour would be: (1) victimisation *by* the company; (2) victimisation *against* the company; (3) victimisation *within* the company'. (Our translation). Saad-Diniz (2019), pp. 151–152.

215 Saad-Diniz (2019), p. 152.

What emerges, therefore, as a true scientific challenge is to find the human side hidden in corporate scandals and reposition the victim at the centre of the legitimisation of the criminal justice system, in order to elevate socially harmful corporate behaviour to the status of human rights violator within the scope of companies.[216]

Largely due to the 'business *and* rights' movement (*see above*), the issue has gained greater consistency and greater articulation at an international level, consolidating the idea that, beyond a mere negative duty, the company has a positive duty to promote human rights. As put by Saad-Diniz, the discussion is currently rooted in the formulation of practical alternative means for the prompt and effective remediation of rights violated in the corporate sphere, such as human rights *compliance* and human rights *due diligence*.[217]

References

Books and Theses

Arroyo Zapatero, L., & Nieto Martín, A. (eds) (2013). *El derecho penal económico en la era compliance*. Tirant lo Blanch.
Barrilari, C. (2018b). *Crime empresarial, autorregulação e compliance*. Thomson Reuters.
Bottini PC (2010). *Crimes de perigo abstrato* (2nd rev and updated edn). Revista dos Tribunais.
Deva, S. (2012). *Regulating corporate human rights violations: Humanizing business*. Routledge Research in Human Rights Law.
Geis, G. (2011). *White-collar and corporate crime: A documentary and reference guide*. Greenwood Publishing.
Landman, T., Schudel, C., & Schudel, W. (2007). *Corruption and human rights: Empirical relationships and policy advice*. International Council of Humans Rights.
Laufer, W. S. (2006). *corporate bodies and guilty minds: The failure of corporate criminal liability*. University of Chicago Press.
Piedade ASC (2013). *Criminalidade organizada e dupla face do princípio da proporcionalidade*. PhD Thesis, Pontifical Catholic University.
Rodrigues, A. M. (2019). *Direito penal económico: uma política criminal na era do compliance* (Manuais universitários). Almedina.
Saad-Diniz, E., & Laurentiz, V. (2018). *Corrupção, direitos humanos e empresa*. D'Plácido
Saad-Diniz, E. (2019). Ética negocial e compliance: entre educação executiva e a interpretação judicial. Thomson Reuters Brasil, São Paulo.
Shecaira, S. S. (2020). *Criminologia*. 8th rev, updated and expanded edn. Thomson Reuters Brasil.
Silva Sánchez, J. M. (2013). *A expansão do direito penal: aspectos da política criminal nas sociedades pós-industriais*. Translated by Luiz Otávio de Oliveira Rocha, 3rd edn. Editora Revista dos Tribunais, São Paulo.
Silveira, R. M. J., & Saad-Diniz, E. (2015). *Compliance, direito penal e lei anticorrupção*. Saraiva, São Paulo.
Sutherland, E. H. (1999). *White-collar crime*. La Piqueta.

[216] Saad-Diniz (2019), pp. 184–185.
[217] Saad-Diniz (2019), pp. 187–188.

Tiedemann, K. (1985). *Poder económico y delito: introducción al derecho penal económico y de la empresa* Ariel.
Tiedemann, K. (2009). *derecho penal económico: introducción y parte general*. Librería Jurídica.
Zaffaroni, E. R., & Pierangeli, J. H. (2001). *Manual de direito penal brasileiro: parte geral*. Revista dos Tribunais.

Book Chapters

Arroyo Zapatero, L. (2012). Política criminal y estado de derecho en las sociedades contemporáneas. In Arroyo Zapatero L et al. (Eds.), *Derecho penal de la empresa: Del derecho penal económico del estado social al derecho penal de la empresa globalizado*. Editora Ediar, Buenos Aires.
Barrilari, C. (2018a). Corrupção, empresas e direitos humanos: Diálogo necessário. In E. Saad-Diniz & V. V. Laurentiz (Eds.), *Corrupção, direitos humanos e empresas* D'Plácido Publisher.
Bercovici, G., & Souza, L. A. (2013). Intervencionismo econômico e direito penal mínimo: Uma equação possível. In W. T. Oliveira, et al. (Eds.), *Direito penal econômico: estudos em homenagem aos 75 anos do professor klaus tiedemann* LiberArs.
Bidasolo, M. C. (2008). ¿Cabe limitar la expansión del derecho penal pese a proteger nuevas modalidades delictivas? In E. R. Zaffaroni & K. Tiedemann (Eds.), *Dogmática penal del tercer milenio* ARA Editores.
Costa, G. F. (2011). Breve panorama do pensamento de Edwin H. Sutherland e a nova etiologia da criminalidade. In A. B. G. Souza (Ed.), *Inovações no direito penal econômico: contribuições criminológicas, político-criminais e dogmáticas* ESMPU.
Crespo ED (2018). Vulneración de derechos humanos por empresas multinacionales: ¿De un derecho penal económico transnacional a un derecho penal internacional económico? In E. Crespo & A. Nieto Martín (Eds.), *Derecho penal económico y derechos humanos* Tirant lo Blanch.
Cunha, M. L. R. (2017). A evolução da legislação anticorrupção no Brasil e no mundo. In C. K. Lamboy (Ed.), *Manual de compliance* Instituto ARC.
Francia, M. P. M. (2018). Criminology, economic criminal law and human rights. In E. Crespo & A. Nieto Martín (Eds.), *Economic criminal law and human rights* Tirant lo Blanch.
Francia, M. P. M. (2018). Criminología, derecho penal económico y derechos humanos. In E. Crespo & A. Nieto Martín (Eds.), *Derecho penal económico y derechos humanos* Tirant lo Blanch.
Lascano, C. (2012). Los principios constitucionales del derecho penal económico. Globalización y armonización del derecho penal económico (Mercosur). In L. Arroyo Zapatero, et al. (Ed.), *Derecho penal de la empresa: del derecho penal económico del estado social al derecho penal de la empresa globalizado* Ediar, Buenos Aires.
Lascuraín, J. A. (2018). La responsabilidad penal individual en los delitos de empresa. N. J. Mata Barranco, D. G.-A. J, S. L, & A. Nieto Martín (Eds.), *Derecho penal económico y de la empresa*. Dykinson.
Laufer, W. S. (2019). A explicação ausente da vitimologia. In E. Saad-Diniz (Ed.), *Vitimologia corporativa*. Tirant lo Blanch.
Neves, E. V. P. (2011). A atualidade de Edwin H. Sutherland. In A. B. G. Souza (Ed.), *Inovações no direito penal econômico: contribuições criminológicas, político-criminais e dogmáticas* ESMPU.
Nieto Martín, A. (2018). Introducción al derecho penal económico y de la empresa In A. Nieto Martín, et al. (Ed.), *Derecho Penal Económico Y de la Empresa*.

Nieto Martín, A. (2019a). Compliance, criminologia e responsabilidade penal de pessoas jurídicas. In E. Saad-Diniz & R. Gomes (Eds.), *Manual de cumprimento normativo e responsabilidade das pessoas jurídicas* (2nd ed.). Tirant lo Blanch.

Nieto Martín, A. (2019b). Compliance, criminologia e responsabilidade penal de pessoas jurídicas. In E. Saad-Diniz & R. Gomes (Eds.), *Manual de cumprimento normativo e responsabilidade das pessoas jurídicas* (2nd ed.). Tirant lo Blanch.

Ramassastry, A. (2013). Closing the gap governance in the business and human rights arena: Lessons from the anti-corruption movement. In S. Deva & D. Bilchitz (Eds.), *human rights obligations of business: beyond the corporate responsibility to respect?* Cambridge University Press.

Saad-Diniz, E. (2018). Compliance sob a perspectiva da criminologia econômica. In R. V. B. Cueva & A. Frazão (Eds.), *Compliance: perspectivas e desafios dos programas de conformidade* (p. 175). Fórum.

Sánchez, J. B. (2019). Corporate crime, human rights and human security: Reflections from economic and corporate criminal law. In N. Sans Mulas (Ed.), *Human rights 70 years after the universal declaration* (p. 66). Tirant lo Blanch.

Santos, C. C. (2003). A corrupção: Da luta contra o crime na intersecção de alguns (distintos) entendimentos da doutrina, da jurisprudência e do legislador. In M. C. Andrade (Ed.), *Liber discipulorum para Jorge de Figueiredo Dias* (pp. 963–991). Coimbra Editora.

Silveira, R. M. J. (2012). A busca de legitimidade dos crimes de perigo abstrato no direito penal econômico. *Boletim IBCCRIM*, *20*(238), 6.

Souza, A. B. G. (2011). Da criminologia à política criminal: Direito penal econômico e o novo direito penal. In A. B. G. Souza (Ed.), *Inovações no direito penal econômico: contribuições criminológicas, político-criminais e dogmáticas* (p. 107). ESMPU, Brasília.

Souza, A. B. G. (2021). *Direito penal empresarial: critérios de atribuição de responsabilidade e o papel do compliance*. LiberArs.

Souza, A. B. G., & Coelho, C. C. S. (2021). Criminologia do desvio no ambiente corporativo: A empresa como causa e como cura da corrupção. In F. H. Choukr & C. E. A. Japiassú (Eds.), *Dimensões contemporâneas da atividade empresarial* FACAMP.

Terradillos Basoco, J. M. (2012). Concepto y método del derecho penal económico. In L. Arroyo Zapatero, et al. (Eds.), *Derecho penal de la empresa: del derecho penal económico del estado social al derecho penal de la empresa globalizado* (p. 97). Ediar.

Vogel, J. (2005). Derecho penal y globalización. In Cancio Meliá M (coord.) *Anuario de la Facultad de Derecho de la Universidad Autónoma de Madrid* 9:113–126.

Zaffaroni, E. R. (2015). O papel do direito penal e a crise financeira. In E. Saad-diniz, D. Brodowski, & A. L. B. Sá (Eds.), *Regulação do abuso no âmbito corporativo: o papel do direito penal na crise financeira* (p.13). LiberArs.

Journal and Article

Albanese, J. S. (1984). Corporate criminology: Explaining deviance of business and political organizations. *Journal of Criminal Justice* (12):11–19

Barrilari, C. (2018). Corrupção, empresas e direitos humanos: Diálogo necessário. In E. Saad-Diniz & V. V. Laurentiz (eds.), *Corrupção, direitos humanos e empresas* D'Plácido Publisher.

Bechara, A. E. L. S. (2017). Corrupção, crise política e direito penal: as lições que o Brasil ainda precisa aprender. Boletim IBCCRIM 25(290):05–07.

Bechara, A. E. L. (2020). Criminal law between efficiency and guarantees: reflections of the criminal policy for the control of corruption for the Brazilian criminal system. *Humanities and Rights Global Network Journal* 2(1)

Becker, G. S. (1968). Crime and punishment: an economic approach. *The Journal of Political Economy* 76(2):169–217. https://doi.org/10.1086/259394

Bercovici, G., & Souza, L. A. (2013). Intervencionismo econômico e direito penal mínimo: Uma equação possível. In W. T. Oliveira, et al. (eds.), *Direito penal econômico: estudos em homenagem aos 75 anos do Professor Klaus Tiedemann* LiberArs.

Bidasolo, M. C. (2008). ¿Cabe limitar la expansión del derecho penal pese a proteger nuevas modalidades delictivas? In E. R. Zaffaroni & K. Tiedemann (eds.), *Dogmática penal del tercer milenio* ARA Editores.

Costa, G. F. (2011). Breve panorama do pensamento de Edwin H. Sutherland e a nova etiologia da criminalidade. In A. B. G. Souza (ed.), *Inovações no direito penal econômico: contribuições criminológicas, político-criminais e dogmáticas*. ESMPU.

Crespo ED (2018). Vulneración de derechos humanos por empresas multinacionales: ¿De un derecho penal económico transnacional a un derecho penal internacional económico? In E. Crespo & A. Nieto Martín (eds.), *Derecho penal económico y derechos humanos*. Tirant lo Blanch.

Cunha, M. L. R. (2017). A evolução da legislação anticorrupção no Brasil e no mundo. In C. K. Lamboy (ed.), *Manual de compliance* Instituto ARC.

Francia, M. P. M. (2018) Criminology, economic criminal law and human rights. In E. Crespo & A. Nieto Martín (eds.), *Economic criminal law and human rights*. Tirant lo Blanch.

Francia, M. P. M. (2018). Criminología, derecho penal económico y derechos humanos. In E. Crespo & A. Nieto Martín (eds.), *Derecho penal económico y derechos humanos*. Tirant lo Blanch.

Hess, D. (2017). Business, corruption and human rights: towards a new responsibility for corporations to combat corruption. *Wisconsin Law Review* 2017(4):641–693.

Lascano, C. (2012) Los principios constitucionales del derecho penal económico. Globalización y armonización del derecho penal económico (Mercosur). In L. Arroyo Zapatero, et al. (eds.), *Derecho penal de la empresa: del derecho penal económico del estado social al derecho penal de la empresa globalizado* Ediar.

Lascuraín, J. A. (2018) La responsabilidad penal individual en los delitos de empresa. In N. J. Mata Barranco, D. G.-A. J, S. L, & A. Nieto Martín (eds.), *Derecho penal económico y de la empresa*. Dykinson.

Laufer, W. S. (2019b) A explicação ausente da vitimologia. In E. Saad-Diniz (ed.), *Vitimologia corporativa* Tirant lo Blanch.

Masi, C. V., & Moraes, V. D. L. (2015). Globalização e o direito penal. *Revista Liberdades* 18:16–43.

Neves, E. V. P. (2011). A atualidade de Edwin H. Sutherland. In A. B. G. Souza (ed.), *Inovações no direito penal econômico: contribuições criminológicas, político-criminais e dogmáticas*. ESMPU

Nieto Martín, A. (2018). Introducción al derecho penal económico y de la empresa. In A. Nieto Martín, et al. (eds.), *Derecho penal económico y de la empresa*. Dykinson.

Nieto Martín, A. (2019). Compliance, criminologia e responsabilidade penal de pessoas jurídicas. In E. Saad-Diniz & R. Gomes (eds.), *Manual de cumprimento normativo e responsabilidade das pessoas jurídicas*, 2nd ed. Tirant lo Blanch.

Nieto Martín, A. (2019b). Compliance, criminologia e responsabilidade penal de pessoas jurídicas. In E. Saad-Diniz & R. Gomes (eds.), *Manual de cumprimento normativo e responsabilidade das pessoas jurídicas*, 2nd ed. Tirant lo Blanch

Nieto Martín, A. (2020). Hacia un derecho penal económico europeo de los derechos humanos. *In Dret Penal: Revista para el análisis del derecho* 4:137–172.

Rajagopal, B. (1999). Corruption, legitimacy and human rights: the dialectic of the relationship. *Connecticut Journal of International Law* 14(2).

Ramassastry, A. (2013). Closing the gap governance in the business and human rights arena: Lessons from the anti-corruption movement. In S. Deva & D. Bilchitz (eds.), *Human rights obligations of business: Beyond the corporate responsibility to respect?* Cambridge University Press.

Saad-Diniz, E. (2014). A criminalidade empresarial e a cultura de compliance. *Revista Eletrônica de Direito Penal* 2(2):112–120.

Saad-Diniz, E. (2018). Compliance sob a perspectiva da criminologia econômica. In R. V. B. Cueva & A. Frazão (eds.), *Compliance: perspectivas e desafios dos programas de conformidade* (p 175). Fórum.

Sánchez, J. B. (2019). Corporate crime, human rights and human security: Reflections from economic and corporate criminal law. In N. Sans Mulas (ed.), *human rights 70 years after the universal declaration* (p 66). Tirant lo Blanch.

Santos, C. C. (2003). A corrupção: Da luta contra o crime na intersecção de alguns (distintos) entendimentos da doutrina, da jurisprudência e do legislador. In M. C. Andrade (ed.), *Liber discipulorum para Jorge de Figueiredo Dias* (pp 963–991). Coimbra Editora.

Silveira, R. M. J. (2011) A ideia penal sobre a corrupção no Brasil: da seletividade pretérita à expansão de horizontes atual. *Revista Brasileira de Ciências Criminais* 19(89):407–428.

Silveira, R. M. J. (2012). A busca de legitimidade dos crimes de perigo abstrato no direito penal econômico. *Boletim IBCCRIM 20*(238):6.

Silveira, R. M. J. (2014) A atual percepção sobre o fenômeno da corrupção: questão penal, econômica ou de direitos humanos? *Revista do Advogado* 34(125):131–136.

Souza, A. B. G. (2011). Da criminologia à política criminal: Direito penal econômico e o novo direito penal. In A. B. G. Souza (ed.), *Inovações no direito penal econômico: contribuições criminológicas, político-criminais e dogmáticas* (p 107). ESMPU.

Souza, A. B. G. (2021). *Direito penal empresarial: critérios de atribuição de responsabilidade e o papel do compliance*. LiberArs

Souza, A. B. G., & Coelho, C. C. S. (2021). Criminologia do desvio no ambiente corporativo: A empresa como causa e como cura da corrupção. In F. H. Choukr & C. E. A. Japiassú (eds.), *Dimensões contemporâneas da atividade empresarial*. FACAMP.

Souza, A. B. G., & Japiassú C. E. A. (2017). Criminologia e delinquência empresarial: da cultura criminógena à cultura do compliance. *Quaestio Iuris* 10(2):1031–1051.

Sutherland, E. H. (2014). White-collar criminality. Translated by Lucas Minorelli. *UFRGS Revista Eletrônica de Direito Penal e Política Criminal* 2(2):93–103.

Sykes, G. M., & Matza, D. (1957). Techniques of Neutralization: A theory of Delinquency. *American Sociological Review* 22(6):664–670.

Terradillos Basoco, J. M. (2012). Concepto y método del derecho penal económico. In L. Arroyo Zapatero, et al. (eds.), *Derecho penal de la empresa: del derecho penal económico del estado social al derecho penal de la empresa globalizado* (p. 97). Ediar.

Terradillos Basoco, J. M. (2015) Derecho penal económico. Lineamientos de política penal. *Revista del Instituto de Ciencias Jurídicas de Puebla* 35:7–36

Zaffaroni, E. R. (2015). O papel do direito penal e a crise financeira. In E. Saad-Diniz, D. Brodowski, & A. L. B. Sá (eds.), *Regulação do abuso no âmbito corporativo: o papel do direito penal na crise financeira* (p. 13). LiberArs.

Legal Documents

Brazil, (1988). *Constitution of the Federative republic of Brazil*. Presidency of the republic. Available at: http://www.planalto.gov.br/ccivil_03/Constituicao/Constituicao.htm.

Brazil (2000). *Decree No. 3,678 of 30 November 2000: Promulgates the convention on combating bribery of foreign public officials in international business transactions*. Presidency of the Republic. Available at: http://www.planalto.gov.br/ccivil_03/decreto/d3678.htm.

Brazil (2000). *Decree No. 3,678 of 30 November 2000: Promulgates the convention on combating bribery of foreign public officials in international business transactions (concluded in Paris, 17 December 1997)*. Presidency of the Republic, Brasília. Available at: http://www.planalto.gov.br/ccivil_03/decreto/d3678.htm.

Brazil (2002). *Decree No. 4,410 of 7 October 2002: Promulgates the inter-American convention against corruption (29 March 1996) with reservation for Article XI, paragraph 1*(c). Presidency of the Republic. Available at: http://www.planalto.gov.br/ccivil_03/decreto/2002/d4410.htm.
Brazil (2006). *Decree No. 5,687 of 31 January 2006: Promulgates the United Nations convention against corruption (adopted 31 October 2003)*. Presidency of the Republic. Available at: http://www.planalto.gov.br/ccivil_03/_ato2004.
Council of Europe (1999). *Criminal law convention on corruption* (European Treaty Series No. 173). Council of Europe. Available at: https://rm.coe.int/168007f3f5.
Council of Europe (1999). *Civil law convention on corruption* (European Treaty Series No. 174). Council of Europe. Available at: https://rm.coe.int/168007f3f6.
International Council on Human Rights Policy (2009). *Corruption and human rights: Making the connection*. Elsevier p 3.
Symposium for Young Penalists, 4th (2014) Tema: Regulação do Abuso no Âmbito Corporativo. Associação Internacional de Direito Penal, São Paulo.
United Nations Office on Drugs and Crime (2007). *United nations convention Against corruption*.
United Kingdom (2010). *Bribery Act 2010*. Available at: https://www.legislation.gov.uk/ukpga/2010/23/contents.

Online Sources

Bentes, V. (2021, August 24) Operação Daia: Polícia Federal investiga corrupção e tráfico de influência no DNIT [08:35]. *CNN Brasil*. Available at: https://www.cnnbrasil.com.br/politica/policia-federal-investiga-corrupcao-e-trafico-de-influencia-no-dnit/.
Desidério, M. (2018, September 21) Corruption in Odebrecht is the most organised in the history of capitalism. *Exame*. Available at: https://exame.com/negocios/corrupcao-na-odebrecht-foi-a-mais-organizada-da-historia-do-capitalismo/
Deutsch Welle (2020, July 28) The decline of Odebrecht. *Deutsch Welle*. Available at: https://www.dw.com/pt-br/o-ocaso-da-odebrecht/a-54350923
Drugs and Crime (2007) *United Nations Convention Against Corruption*. United Nations, Brasília.
Época (14 November 2014). https://epoca.oglobo.globo.com/tempo/noticia/2014/09/tudo-para-entender-bo-caso-petrobrasb.html.
Estadão (2015, 9 November) *Os maiores escândalos corporativos do século 21* [17:15]. Available at: https://economia.estadao.com.br/galerias/geral,os-maiores-escandalos-corporativos-do-seculo-21,22419
FATF (2012). *International standards on combating money laundering and the financing of terrorism & proliferation: The FATF recommendations* (trans: Salles D). COAF. Available at: https://www.fatf-gafi.org/media/fatf/documents/recommendations/pdfs/FATF-40-Rec-2012-Portuguese-GAFISUD.pdf
G1 (2015, 23 September) Escândalo da Volkswagen: Veja o passo a passo do caso [15:48]. *G1*. Available at: http://g1.globo.com/carros/noticia/2015/09/escandalo-da-volkswagen-veja-o-passo-passo-do-caso.html
Gara, A. (2015, 28 September) The 10 biggest frauds in recent US history. *Forbes*. Available at: https://forbes.com.br/fotos/2015/09/10-maiores-fraudes-da-historia-recente-dos-estados-unidos/#foto3
Institute for Human Rights and Business (2019). *Building a movement: Reflections on the history and future of business and human rights*. p. 1.
International Council on Human Rights Policy (2009) *Corruption and Human Rights: Making the Connection*. Elsevier p 3.

Ministério da Justiça e Segurança Pública (2019). *[Title of specific content]*. Available at: https://www.justica.gov.br/news/collective-nitf-content-1554990835.08

Ministério Público Federal (2021). *Entenda o caso*. Available at: http://www.mpf.mp.br/grandes-casos/lava-jato/entenda-o-caso

Ministério Público Federal (2021). *Understand the case*. Available at: http://www.mpf.mp.br/grandes-casos/lava-jato/entenda-o-caso

Organization of American States (1996). *Inter-American Convention Against Corruption*. OAS, Caracas. Available at: http://www.oas.org/juridico/portuguese/treaties/b-58.htm

Passarinho, N. (2019, February 13) *Fiscalização de barragens: órgão federal é o 2º mais exposto a fraudes e corrupção, diz TCU*. BBC News Brasil. Available at: https://www.bbc.com/portuguese/brasil-47211131

Pozzi, S. (2018, May 4). *US sues former Volkswagen CEO over 'Dieselgate'* [22:44]. *El País*. Available at: https://brasil.elpais.com/noticias/caso-volkswagen/

Stop Corporate Impunity. Stop Corporate Impunity (2021). *Stop corporate impunity*. Available at: https://www.stopcorporateimpunity.org/?lang=pt-br

Terra (2016, December 22). Odebrecht: Understand the biggest bribery case in history. *Terra*. Available at: https://www.terra.com.br/noticias/brasil/odebrecht-entenda-o-maior-caso-de-suborno-da-historia,2ad4c9f40bf9d93e1b2fba08935c112cokpstq92.html

Transparency International (2022). *Toolkits for business*. Available at: https://www.transparency.org/en/toolkits/business

Tribunal de Contas da União (2019). *Subsídios técnicos para a comissão externa do desastre de Brumadinho*. TCU, Brasília. Available at: https://portal.tcu.gov.br/data/files/40/80/3B/09/B7A1F6107AD96FE6F18818A8/Subsidios_tecnicos_comissao_externa_desastre_Brumadinho.pdf

United Nations General Assembly (1976). *Measures against corrupt practices of transnational and other corporations, their intermediaries and others involved*. UN. Available at: https://digitallibrary.un.org/record/189574

United States Department of Justice (2017). *Foreign Corrupt Practices Act*. Available at: https://www.justice.gov/criminal-fraud/foreign-corrupt-practices-act

Veja (2014, April 18). Polícia Federal investigará Eike por fraude na OGX [17:18]. *Veja*. Available at: https://veja.abril.com.br/economia/policia-federal-investigara-eike-por-fraude-na-ogx/

Chapter 4
Criminal Compliance and Corporate Criminal Liability: Perspectives for Preventive Protection of Human Rights in the Corporate Sphere

From the outlines of the previous section, it is possible to identify some guiding principles that, in summary, point to: (i) the increasingly evident context of corporate activities involved in illicit practices, such as corruption, leading to a growing search for containment mechanisms; (ii) the expanding reality of criminal law in an attempt to provide answers to economic crime, often revealing itself as an inadequate tool for such a task; (iii) the essentiality of criminological contributions to the construction of combat tools, whether for corporate crime itself or for prevention and restoration in victimology resulting from socially harmful corporate behaviour.

Within this complex and multidisciplinary context of ideas, the analysis of compliance programmes and potential corporate criminal liability for illicit deviations is proposed, focusing on the indispensable and necessary prevention of corporate violations of human rights.

4.1 Self-Regulation and Compliance Programmes

In response to major financial scandals and the aim of de-regulating activities carried out by economic agents, along with the considerable resulting social damage,[1] the proposal for regulated self-regulation emerged, from which the guidelines for corporate governance and compliance[2] were established. In a globalised world,

[1] Complementing the idea: 'The programmes of *compliance* and the new forms of regulation for the prevention of related crime are a reaction to the spectacular financial scandals in the field of economic crime experienced recently both in the USA and in Europe [. . .], which since then have already indicated the basis that economic crime could lead to both bankruptcy and considerable damage to society as a whole'. (Our translation). Sieber (2013), p. 291.

[2] Rodrigues (2019), p. 45.

L. d. B. Ibarra Papa, *Prevention of Human Rights Violations in the Corporate Sphere*, IBCCrim Studies in Criminal Law, Human Rights and Criminology 1,
https://doi.org/10.1007/978-3-032-06213-0_4

where the regulatory and sanctioning capacity of states in relation to economic activity is significantly weakened, regulatory compliance is a tool of global governance or global law.[3]

On this basis, formulas for co-regulation between the state and private companies are established, primarily aimed at preventing illicit activities such as corruption. Under this example, one can even speak of a privatisation of the fight against corruption as a change in prevention strategy, also betting on companies as agents in the fight against corruption.[4] Therefore, a new emerging reality is seen in which self-regulation intertwines with criminal politics.[5]

Measures of self-control and crime prevention originated in the United States during the policies of privatisation and deregulation of economic sectors, at which point, the need for new criminal-political strategies for a type of state no longer directly interventionist was realised.[6]

In this context, as posed by Nieto Martín:[7] how can compliance with state regulatory provisions be effectively ensured? How can the effectiveness of enforcement in complying with these rules be guaranteed if companies, as global entities, are operating in various territories, or even when corporations surpass the state itself?

Ulrich Sieber notes three forms or 'models' of socio-economic regulation, which can occur through (i) exclusive regulation of each economic sector (self-regulation), with a large margin of freedom for companies; (ii) pure state regulation (heteroregulation), which sets all determining decisions; and (iii) public-private co-regulation (regulated self-regulation), in a joint action by the state and private initiative.[8]

As for the latter—which is most relevant to this work—there is a coupling between state law and private systems, characterised by 'the fact that state provisions create more or less detailed precepts or create structures that encourage self-regulation or make self-regulation measures binding'.[9] Indeed, it is essential to reiterate that the adoption of regulated self-regulation comes, as stated, from its selection among models of state intervention in economic activity,[10] in order to overcome the increasingly evident insufficiency of the State to exercise its due

[3] Nieto Martín (2013b), p. 172.

[4] 'La política criminal más reciente ha responsabilizado también a las empresas em la lucha contra la corrupción. La moderna política pública de lucha contra la corrupción se caracteriza porque: (a) exigen a las empresas que adopten medidas internas de prevención de la corrupción y que ayuden al Estado—a sus policías, jueces y fiscales—en la investigación y esclarecimiento de los casos de corrupción; [. . .]' Nieto Martín (2013a), p. 134.

[5] Silveira and Saad-Diniz (2015), p. 68.

[6] Souza (2015), pp. 124–125.

[7] Arroyo Zapatero and Nieto Martín (eds) (2013).

[8] Sieber (2013), p. 292.

[9] Souza (2021), p. 62.

[10] Souza (2021), p. 62.

control, notably in the face of technological advancement and its implications in the business field.[11]

In this paradigm shift, there is talk of a confluence of actors, with the use of normative tools from *hard law, soft law* and private self-regulation[12] (see Chap. 2). There is talk of a new model of public interventionism, which is based on cooperation between public powers, regulated subjects (companies) and other social agents (e.g. international organisations), in order to ensure a more effective presence of the State, in a form of more sophisticated social control.[13] Ian Ayres and John Braithwaite, in a metaregulatory theory, note this new control as *responsive regulation,*[14] in the sense that 'public regulation can promote the governance of the private market through enlightened delegations of regulatory functions'.[15]

The authors point out methodologies for the constitution of *win-win* solutions in the *regulation game* between public and private *players,*[16] in functional cooperation,[17] to adopt a model of *enforced self-regulation,*[18] which translates the negotiation between the State and companies in order to oblige them to establish their own regulatory standards (*tailor-made*) with the aim of avoiding more severe and less adaptable state standards to the individual reality of the company (*less tailored*).[19]

Regarding *(government) enforced self-regulation (of illegal corporate conduct)* or regulated/forced self-regulation, already in the 1980s, Braithwaite, foreseeing the failure of the justice system and regulatory agencies in controlling economic crime and drawing from the idea that corporations are more capable than the State of regulating their own commercial activities, proposed that companies create

---

[11] Silveira and Saad-Diniz (2015), p. 70.

[12] Nieto Martín (2013a), p. 134.

[13] Rodrigues (2019), p. 46.

[14] 'The enforced self-regulation model presented [. . .] is about negotiation occurring between the state and individual firms to establish regulations that are particularised to each firm. Each firm in an industry is required to propose its own regulatory standards if it is to avoid harsher (and less tailored) standards imposed by the state. This individual-firm, as opposed to industry-association, self-regulation is "enforced" in two senses. First, the firm is required by the state to do the self-regulation. Second, the privately written rules can be publicly enforced. Enforced self-regulation is, therefore, a more radically innovative proposal than co-regulation, although the two are functionally equivalent in the pyramid analysis as intermediate strategies'. Ayres and Braithwaite (1992), p. 101.

[15] The authors mention: 'We have seen that corporations may be more capable than the government of regulating their business activities. But if they are more capable, they are not necessarily more willing to regulate effectively. This is the fundamental weakness of voluntary self-regulation [. . .]. Enforced self-regulation, on the other hand, can ensure that internal compliance groups will not be lightly overruled. [. . .] Thus, enforced self-regulation combines the versatility and flexibility of voluntary self-regulation, but avoids many of the inherent weaknesses of voluntarism'. Ayres and Braithwaite (1992), pp. 105–106.

[16] Ayres and Braithwaite (1992), p. 17.

[17] Sieber (2013), p. 300.

[18] Also known as *'at-a-distance forms of state regulation'*.

[19] Ayres and Braithwaite (1992), p. 101.

their prevention programmes under the 'supervision' of the State (*new regulatory state*)[20] in order to ensure that internal compliance groups are not lightly ignored, as they are in the voluntary *self-regulation* model.[21]

In summary, Anabela Miranda presents regulated self-regulation as being 'the subordination of the self-regulation of the private entity to the ends and state interests', in a transfer of competences that previously belonged exclusively to the States and that has now been outsourced or privatised. From this, it is up to companies to also carry out the prevention, investigation, prosecution and repression of illicit and criminal conduct.[22] In this system, on the other hand, it is up to the State to define the rules of regulation, which include various normative possibilities of *enforcement*, such as, anti-corruption *compliance* programmes[23] and risk prevention in the labour field, in the financial market, in consumer protection, in the environment and in money laundering.[24]

Therefore, the State, having control over corporate self-regulation,[25] considers the possibility of the *jus puniendi* acting as a source of *enforcement,* since, given the possibility of applying criminal sanctions to corporate offences, it promotes the incentive for company directors to establish more effective control mechanisms, notably motivated by the desire to obtain mitigations or even exemptions when applying their criminal liability, as is currently the case in the Spanish Penal Code (Art. 31 bis, No. 2 and 4).[26]

These circumstances are pointed out by the doctrine as the 'stick and carrot' approach; that is, companies tend to envisage and opt for the possibility of a shorter period of discomfort/liability (*stick*) due to a longer period of easing/reintegration (*carrot*). In other words, the punished are encouraged to cooperate with their punishers during their *stick period.*[27]

In summary, the idea is that *super-punishment* encourages the cooperation of punished companies and also disinhibits them from self-punishing (*self-punishment*) in the sense of contributing to cooperation, because 'by cooperating, the punished company can move more quickly from the more painful *stick* to the

[20] Braithwaite (2000) The new regulatory state. *Br J Criminol* 40:222–238. On another occasion, the author exemplifies: 'Under enforced self-regulation, the government would compel each company to write a set of rules tailored to the unique set of contingencies facing that firm. A regulatory agency would either approve these rules or send them back for revision if they were insufficiently stringent'. Braithwaite (1982), p. 1470.

[21] Braithwaite (1982), pp. 1468–1470.

[22] Rodrigues (2019), p. 49.

[23] Rodrigues (2019), p. 49.

[24] Nieto Martín (2008), p. 2.

[25] To complement this idea of self-regulation: '[…] through which administrative regulations encourage companies to adopt certain organisational rules aimed at complementing both the normative function of the State, as well as its policing and sanctioning function'. (Our translation). Nieto (2008), p. 3.

[26] Rodrigues (2019), p. 50.

[27] Ayres and Braithwaite (1992), p. 43.

less painful *carrot*'.[28] In addition, 'super-punishments can be useful for agencies seeking regulatory compliance'.[29]

This is why, as Ulrich Sieber mentions,[30] companies and legislators/regulators around the world have developed new concepts for enhancing ethical values in company management and preventing corporate crime, the most common concepts being: 'compliance programme', 'risk management', 'value management' and 'corporate governance', as well as 'business ethics', 'integrity codes', 'codes of conduct' and 'corporate social responsibility (CSR)'.

As Adán Nieto Martín points out, the importance of the rapid dissemination of the concept of corporate governance has three foundations arising from market pressure (notably the American one): (i) international convergence of law from the American model, (ii) attraction of investors when there is confidence in knowing that the companies in which they operate are properly managed and controlled, and that there is containment of the abuse of power by the management body and (iii) counter-reaction to the financial scandals that shook the American economy during the turn of the century.[31]

At this point, it cannot be denied that the culture of good governance has been incorporated into the political-criminal source of prevention of economic crime, which is why understanding the concepts becomes fundamental in the debate, especially in the context of economic criminal law.

4.1.1 Aspects of Corporate Governance

Although the concepts of *corporate governance* and their relationship with the programmes of *compliance* yield considerable propositions and approaches, the aim here is to theoretically elucidate,[32] within the limits set by this work, the processes of development, as well as to establish the direction of the implementation of these concepts in the business reality, so as to serve as tools for the political and dogmatic-criminal approaches that will follow.

[28] Ayres and Braithwaite (1992), p. 43.

[29] Furthermore, in addition: 'By cooperating with punishment on one charge, the defendant may get the carrot of immunity from further prosecution on other, more serious, charges. If defendants "take their medicine", they can more quickly move to the carrot period of reintegration. If they do not, instead of stick-carrot, they get stick and more stick'. Ayres and Braithwaite (1992), p. 43.

[30] Sieber (2013), p. 292.

[31] Nieto Martín (2007), p. 120–135.

[32] It is essential to clarify that the ideas presented here tend to address the topics in a more theoretical and less practical way. The importance of practical digressions to the effective implementation of corporate governance and compliance programmes is not overlooked, however, the proposal of the work is to present the theoretical panorama and inferences about the concepts as institutes evaluated by the Science of Law.

In line with the ideas of the previous topic, the panorama of the development of corporate governance and *compliance* reaches a great amplitude both within the framework of *deregulation* and in the process of globalisation and internationalisation of markets (see Topic 2.2). This occurs because of the collision between the interests of shareholders and investors and those of corporate management, as well as between these and the employees, collaborators, suppliers and residents of the communities where the economic activity actually takes place (e.g. *host states*). For the former, only the return rates of the investment made are of interest, while 'for the latter, in an ideal plan, the social engagement of activity is of interest, or, in a more realistic plan, the satisfaction of their own immediate interests'.[33]

To complement such inferences, it is understood that the relationships generated by the legal entity can be seen from two different angles: (i) from an internal angle, which looks at the relationships established between the owners and the managers of the company; (ii) from an external angle, which focuses on the company's relationships with those around it. Thus, in the first case, it is about the conflict between *shareholders* and administrators. In the second case, it is about what is established between *stakeholders* and the company.[34]

Adán Nieto Martín,[35] in a distinct synthesis, establishes that good corporate governance—namely, corporate governance—must involve checks and balances in order to cumulatively address issues related to the first aspect, with the aim of avoiding abuses of power by both the board of directors and the company's management, as well as issues related to the second aspect, in order to reconcile the interests of the company with its surroundings, which is the proper field of CSR.

The author points out,[36] then, the measures to be adopted in this new era of the corporate world, the first element being the need for companies to establish their norms of behaviour or compliance (*compliance*), specifying principles that may have been legally set in a generic way, in order to reconcile the statements in light of their different particularities (again the idea of *tailor-made*). These norms are incorporated into instruments such as codes of conduct, good governance codes and codes of good technical and ethical practices.[37]

The second element is the improvement of information systems, both those intended for the circulation of information within the corporation and those that establish communication channels with the outside (e.g. authorities, consumers, shareholders and investors). In the framework of good corporate governance, where administrators can efficiently exercise their supervisory and oversight

---

[33] Sarcedo (2014), p. 51.

[34] Barrilari (2018), p. 90.

[35] Nieto (2008), p. 2.

[36] It is pertinent to note that, on this occasion, the paths of the aforementioned author were adopted, however, it is not forgotten that the topic has countless sources of thought, which, in general terms, converge to what is succinctly being indicated.

[37] Nieto (2008), p. 5.

functions in an informed manner, the presence of two aspects is fundamental: (i) the imposition of documentation duty norms regarding possible illicit occurrences, as a way for the company to generate evidential material to more easily locate, if necessary, the person responsible for the infraction; and (ii) the presence of *whistleblowers* or informants.[38]

A third element or characteristic is institutionalisation, or, in other words, the tendency of the company to reflect these new norms of conduct throughout its structure, appointing people or bodies whose specific task is to ensure the effectiveness of the organisation in regulatory compliance. These are the *compliance* bodies or departments.[39]

The fourth characteristic of good governance systems is the requirement for the existence of an external control that ensures the effectiveness of the norms (*enforcement*) by certifying, evaluating or auditing the adequacy of self-regulation. There may be audits of different matters, e.g. accounting, criminal, labour, environmental and social.[40]

Under all these elements/practices of corporate governance within the framework of *enforced self-regulation*, it is emphasised that it is not about giving broad freedom to private entities, but rather ensuring that regulations are more particularised and therefore more efficient, so as to prevent state intervention from being dysfunctional. Thus, what characterises modern self-regulation is a distinct intervention, less coercive and more dialogic, with *ex-ante* authorisations or *ex-post* supervision of the model adopted by the company.[41]

Self-regulation becomes even more dialogic when it allows the participation of interested third parties, who, individually or collectively, are affected by the business activities carried out.[42] The barriers between the internal and external aspects of companies are increasingly flexible and interpenetrating, notably 'because the decisions made internally have the potential to affect the entire surroundings of the company, what the company adopts as value will generate a corporate culture to be passed on to external relations'.[43]

These ideas are notable when intending to combine preventive efforts with the protection of human rights in the corporate field.

With this foundation of ideas, the concept of corporate governance[44] can be established from its main objective, which is to create an efficient set of mechanisms or controls for both incentives and monitoring in order to ensure that 'the behaviour of executives is always aligned with the interest of the *shareholders*,

[38] Nieto (2008), pp. 6–7.

[39] Nieto (2008), pp. 6–7.

[40] Nieto (2008), p. 7.

[41] Nieto (2008), p. 8.

[42] Nieto (2008), pp. 8–9.

[43] Barrilari (2018), p. 90.

[44] Anabela Miranda warns that the concept of *corporate governance* is difficult to define, being polyhedral and complex, but, generally, among the various possible definitions, the common point is the aim to address various concerns, aligning conflicting interests. Rodrigues (2019), p. 52.

providing owners, shareholders and quota holders with the monitoring of the company's administration and the tracking of the results of its management'.[45]

In view of this set of diversities in which it is inserted, the concept of corporate governance has been developed in the sense that all business practices are oriented according to four major value pillars: *fairness, disclosure, accountability* and *compliance.*[46]

Fairness, or the need for justice and equity in relation to minority shareholders, refers to the guarantee of equal participation in the company's results and effective participation in assemblies. *Disclosure* refers to the need for transparency in corporate information, especially information of great relevance, considered as such when it reflects on the company's results or involves business risks or opportunities. *Accountability* emphasises the need for responsible accountability, based on the best accounting and auditing techniques. Finally, *compliance* is associated with conformity and adherence to regulatory norms, as expressed in corporate statutes, internal regulations and normative instruments applicable to companies and their activities.[47]

Despite the essentiality of all these value pillars of *corporate governance,*[48] *compliance* is the object of greatest relevance in this work, which is why the following lines are directed to its study, without disregarding that the others also touch on the theme.

4.1.2 Compliance Programmes and Criminal Sciences: The Formulation of Criminal Compliance and the Search for Effectiveness

Before further developing the concept of *compliance*, it is important to point out that there is difficulty in finding a linguistic equivalent that can convey the holistic meaning of the term. In Brazil, synonyms such as 'compliance', 'conformity' and 'integrity' are commonly adopted,[49] these provisions are used in this work as concepts that denote the same central idea.

The term *compliance,* or normative compliance—the latter frequently used in the Spanish language—, means what is most evident: to act in accordance with legality, in a broad sense, in the fulfilment of obligations arising from the law

---

[45] Sarcedo (2014), p. 52.

[46] Rodrigues (2019), p. 54.

[47] Sarcedo (2014), p. 54.

[48] Just to complement the concept of corporate governance: 'referring to the North American model, three pillars are identified on which effective company management should be based: *governance, risk management and compliance* (GRC). Its origin is rooted in the *Principles of Corporate Governance* outlined by the *American Law Institute*, which inspire the majority of good governance rules developed'. (Our translation). Rodrigues (2019), p. 54.

[49] Souza (2021), p. 74.

(civil, administrative, labour, criminal, etc.) and the internal guidelines of the company,[50] that is, as a measure of control or self-monitoring.[51]

It is clear that the concept, by itself, does not guarantee the exercise of compliance (*to comply*), being, at first glance, a goal of the company to be achieved. In this sense, its action paths clearly demand a management tool, an instrument to bring life to the concept. The programmes of *compliance,* of normative fulfilment or integrity (as referred to in Brazilian legislation) perform this task by preventing illicit/irregular behaviours and, when these occur, through their detection and due sanction.[52]

On the other hand, the concept of *compliance* can be understood in light of the inferences brought by corporate governance, complemented by the understanding of CSR and business ethics, in order to meet current demands for integrity and respect not only in its own business but also in the social environment in which it is inserted.[53]

It is for no other reason that it is said to be the *compliance*, a methodologically multidisciplinary concept,[54] which requires the convergence of various approaches and legal frameworks[55] in order to put it into practice. The internal rules that make up the *compliance* programmes are similar to *'a kind of large river into which numerous tributaries of very different origins flow'*.[56]

It can be said, then, that *compliance* coexists in the business environment with a series of movements or related phenomena, to which it is so closely related that it has, to a large extent, a symbiotic or feedback relationship between means and ends. These are phenomena such as, self-regulation, business ethics, codes of conduct, *risk management,* CSR,[57] ISO standards and certifications,[58] COSO,[59] etc.[60]

---

[50] Nieto Martín (2019b), p. 30.

[51] Souza (2015), pp. 124–126.

[52] Nieto Martín (2019b), p. 30.

[53] Barrilari (2019), p. 57.

[54] Nieto Martín (2022), p. 6.

[55] Detailed in: Nieto Martín (2022), p. 7–11.

[56] Nieto Martín (2013b), p. 172.

[57] If it were possible to define it: 'CSR, at least as it is predominantly understood today, implies a new vision of the company, the company as a responsible citizen (*good citizens corporations*), as an act not only economic, but also social and political, with obligations towards its community'. (Our translation). Nieto Martín (2019b), p. 45.

[58] The abbreviation ISO comes from the so-called International Organization of Standardization, which develops, publishes and certifies international standards of quality, organisation, security, etc. For more details: ISO standards are internationally agreed by experts. *iso.org*. Available at: International Organization for Standardization (2025) ISO standards. https://www.iso.org/standards.html.

[59] The abbreviation COSO originates from the Committee of Sponsoring Organizations of the Treadway Commission, which aims to improve business performance, with the development of internal control mechanisms, risk assessment, governance and fraud prevention mechanisms in the company's internal processes etc. It is largely recognised for its methods and work structures (*frameworks*), the most used in this field of analysis being the cubic structural model Enterprise Risk Management—Integrated Framework. For more details: International Organization for Standardization (2025) ISO standards. https://www.iso.org/standards.html.

[60] Nieto Martín (2019b), p. 40.

These instruments deal, then, with the creation, implementation and supervision of codes of conduct with the purpose of generating awareness about duties and obligations in the prevention of legal and regulatory risks inherent to the activity developed, e.g. tax, social security, competition, labour, occupational safety, environmental, among others. When the risks involved permeate the practice of crimes and deal with the possibility of criminal liability, we speak of *criminal compliance*.[61]

Notably in the criminal field—which, in this work, is the main focus—one can question what the role of criminal law is in relation to forms of corporate self-regulation and, notably, in relation to *compliance*. In this sense, questions are pointed out to two sides of the same coin. On one side, what criminal content should be introduced into the system of rules and internal procedures of companies? On the other side, how does *compliance* contribute to criminal law?[62]

There is a fundamental starting point to these questions that relates to the fact that criminal law '*has been the last guest to this corporate party of self-regulation*', [63] and, therefore, it is symptomatic that the sources already used as implementation lines often coincide with specifically criminal provisions, such as Chap. 8 of the *Guidelines*.[64] In this way, *criminal compliance* involves organising all these sources already initially used in the formulation of the concept of normative compliance and interpreting them using a *Denkbrillen* (thinking glasses) of the criminalist, in order to insert a new element of compliance into this already constructed normative field: criminal law.[65]

Indeed, it is pertinent to point out that the rules of economic criminal law are accessories to all the precepts of *compliance*, so that the task of companies in *criminal compliance* is not to specifically comply with criminal law to avoid liability, but rather to directly comply with criminal laws from their codes of conduct, which delimit the perimeter of prohibited behaviour up to where '*la ley no llega*' or even go '*más allá de la ley*', prohibiting behaviours that are in the area prior to criminal types.[66] It is not for another reason that extrapenal prevention

---

[61] Sarcedo (2014), p. 56.

[62] Nieto Martín (2013b), p. 172.

[63] Nieto Martín (2013b), p. 172.

[64] Nieto Martín (2013b), p. 177. Specifically regarding the Guidelines (as already seen in *previous sections*), see the OECD Guidelines for Multinational Enterprises. Its Chap. 8 pertains to 'Combating corruption, solicitation of bribery and extortion'. OECD (2011) OECD Guidelines for Multinational Enterprises. OECD Publishing, Paris.

[65] Nieto Martín (2013b), p. 178.

[66] To complement, the author mentions: 'El criminal compliance no consiste en asesorar a la empresa para que establezca una normativa interna que le permita moverse en el filo de la navaja, sino para que cumpla con lo dispuesto en los códigos éticos. Por esta razón, al compliance no le interesan necesariamente los complejos debates del derecho penal económico acerca de si la conducta A es típica o constituye otro tipo de ilícito. El cumplimiento normativo debe comenzar normalmente mucho antes del tipo penal. Esta forma de entender el cumplimiento normativo es especialmente útil para empresas multinacionales que actúan en varios ordenamientos'. Nieto Martín (2013b), p. 178.

norms developed by self-regulation can be assumed as the basis of the character of *ultima ratio* of criminal law.[67]

In this respect, if self-imposed premises can limit the scope of Criminal Law, prompting its reassignment to the ideal field of *ultima ratio*, in coherence with its liberal claim, 'there may need to be a variation in the very idea of social control traditionally attributed to Criminal Law'.[68]

Furthermore, criminal sciences can greatly contribute to improving *compliance* systems, especially through the inferences brought by economic criminology. This is because criminal prevention strategies in *compliance* programmes, traditionally directed at the function of preventing and detecting criminal acts, if criminologically oriented, can designate them as means of social control, preventing deviant behaviours within an organisation.[69]

Indeed, prevention methods can deter certain points of convergence with some criminological theories of crime prevention, in such a way that they can assume more sophisticated commitments in the instaurations of criminal programmes, directing them, above all, to community prevention (with the reinforcement of the company's ethical values, the strengthening of the community-company's compliance culture, the assumption of an active attitude towards the reported crime) and the adoption of neutralisation techniques.[70] In this sense, 'the theoretical justifications of economic criminality and the related measures of "reinforcing normative compliance standards" must take into account a plurality of factors and motivations that lead to economic infractions'.[71]

Consider, for example, the already-mentioned theory of opportunity (see Item 3.2.1), which shows a certain affinity with the implementation of *compliance* programmes, since the understanding of the probabilities of occurrence of economic infractions—that is, of motivation, the victim's profile, spaces free of effective control—and the company's own routine[72] tends to favour the increase in the development of preventive strategies, minimising the structure of opportunities for the commission of crimes. In the words of Nieto Martín,[73] 'the structure of opportunities should be realised in the most concrete way possible', analysing the concrete structures of the appearance of crimes (e.g. corruption with the aim of winning or obtaining a public contract), 'to, from there, analyse the different routines, spaces or procedures in which there is a possibility of contact between the possible author and the object of the crime' (e.g. procedures in tenders).

Furthermore, a point of relevance to criminal law is the perspective that, if the concept of *risk assessment* is translated into the language of criminology, this

---

[67] Nieto Martín (2013b), p. 178.

[68] Silveira and Saad-Diniz (2015), p. 72.

[69] Nieto Martín (2013b), p. 180.

[70] Nieto Martín (2013b), p. 180.

[71] Saad-Diniz (2019), p. 124.

[72] Saad-Diniz (2019), p. 125.

[73] Nieto Martín (2019a), p. 72.

stage of the compliance programme would be equivalent to uncovering the aetiological facts of criminal behaviour within the company, whether at the individual level (directors' degree of risk aversion) or collective level (market pressure, remuneration system that encourages the pursuit of short-term benefits, criminal group spirit, etc.).[74]

Added to this aspect are the behavioural sciences, such as social psychology or pedagogy, which assist, along with criminological analysis, in the development of training programmes that 'can enhance moral reasoning, appropriately select personnel to operate in a hazardous environment or, more generally, understand the facts that lead to deviant behaviour'.[75] This is what is now referred to as *behavioural compliance.*

In any case, it is understood that the immediate aim of *compliance* programmes is indeed the promotion of an ethical business culture and compliance, but it cannot be denied that their main objective is to avoid administrative, civil and, ultimately, criminal liability,[76] not to mention the severe damage to the company's reputation and market value.[77]

Be that as it may, it is worth noting that local or global costs appear to be so severe as to require corporate ethical controls, serving as a 'new firmament of corporate culture', which allows for 'verifying the possibility of building a new Criminal Law within a new preventive framework, or, truly, a Criminal Law focused on *criminal compliance'*.[78]

With this new scenario given to criminal sciences in mind, and invited to participate in the formulation of corporate self-regulation, it is appropriate to point out the verifiable objects within the programmes, although it is not possible to determine, in abstract, the exact content of the *compliance* programmes, especially due to the need to implement a personalised programme suitable for

[74] He aptly mentions that: '*El plan de estudios ideal para la formación de compliance officer, del oficial de ética o de cualquier persona que quiera dedicarse profesionalmente al cumplimiento normativo, sería una mezcla de criminología con conocimientos de auditoría y management empresarial'*. Nieto Martín (2013b) Fundamental problems of regulatory compliance in criminal law. In: Llamacponcca Mendonza F (ed), p. 180.

[75] Nieto Martín (2022), p. 7.

[76] Rodrigues (2019), p. 57.

[77] Sarcedo (2014), p. 58. In a practical way, recent cases are recalled about the binomial corporate scandals vs. market value: (i) Facebook and the data leak of users, see more at: the scandal that made Facebook lose US$ 35 billion in hours. *BBC News*, 20 Mar, 2018. BBC News (2018) the scandal that made Facebook lose US$35 billion in hours. https://www.bbc.com/portuguese/internacional-43466255. Accessed April 2025.; (ii) Case of JBS and Operation Weak Meat, see more at: Estadão (2017) JBS shares fall 11% after Operation Weak Meat. https://economia.estadao.com.br/noticias/geral,acoes-da-jbs-e-da-brf-devem-ser-penalizadas-pela-operacao-carne-fraca,70001703746. Accessed April 2025; (iii) Carrefour and the murder of a black man in one of its establishments, see more at: Moura (2020) Carrefour shares fall more than 5% after murder of black man. *Folha de S. Paulo*, 23 November. *https://www1.folha.uol.com.br/mercado/2020/11/acoes-do-carrefour-caem-mais-de-5-apos-assassinato-de-homem-negroshtml.* Accessed April 2025.

[78] Silveira RMJ, p. 74.

the reality of that corporation, taking into account the organisational structure or size of the company.[79]

Notwithstanding this, it is possible to identify a common denominator in self-regulation systems. Thus, in general, compliance programmes have regulatory components: prevention, investigation and sanctioning[80] or, put in other words, the structures of *compliance* must be capable of identifying, evaluating, monitoring, controlling and mitigating operational risks.[81]

From these general components, common elements can be identified in the basic structure of all *compliance* programmes and, in this case, in *criminal compliance.*

In the *formulation* phase of the programme,[82] the first step is to identify and analyse the risks involved in the company's activities, with the primary purpose of detecting the most likely offences, the most affected sectors of activity and the effectiveness of any existing control measures.[83] From these outlines, the creation and adoption of a code of ethics or conduct and company policies are initiated, in which the subjects and behavioural expectations are presented in more detail, especially aimed at encompassing mitigating measures for those criminal risks identified.[84]

Still in this phase, mechanisms are formulated that allow the identification of deviant behaviours, considering notably the definition of competencies of control agents.[85] It can be said, in summary, that at this inaugural moment, the aim is to foresee and adopt policies not only of prevention but also of solution, repair or fixing of situations (risks) not filtered by preventive structures.[86] This is a phase of *control,* so it is not enough to simply instruct the members of the organisation on how they should behave, but it is essential to establish measures that ensure the norms will be complied with, and the format can vary depending on the crime that is to be prevented.[87]

At the time of *implementation,* it is about ensuring the communication-promotion -organisation vectors of the programme, which is, guaranteeing, in each segment of administrators' and employees' actions, the knowledge of the codes and procedures formulated so that the culture of compliance with the constructed norms is implemented.[88] This involves *education, training and communication* with the aim

[79] Rodrigues (2019), p. 57.

[80] Rodrigues (2019), p. 58.

[81] Sarcedo (2014), p. 58.

[82] Rodrigues (2019), p. 58.

[83] Nieto Martín (2019a), p. 149.

[84] Nieto Martín (2019a), p. 149.

[85] Rodrigues (2019), p. 58.

[86] Sarcedo (2014), p. 56.

[87] 'As examples of controls, we can mention the structuring of internal processes according to the "four eyes" principle, that is, always a minimum of two people to verify and approve transactions, staff selection, payment control and payment instruments, the *due diligence* at the time of hiring consultants and commercial representatives etc'. (Our translation). Nieto Martín (2019a), p. 150.

[88] Rodrigues (2019), p. 58.

of equipping and training all operators to fulfil their roles consistently with the programme, as well as formulating efficient and accessible communication mechanisms, whether for the dissemination of norms or for access to information and solutions to any difficulties encountered.[89]

In the third phase of *consolidation*—which involves reacting, sanctioning and improving—it is fundamental to include sanctioning mechanisms capable of reacting to illicit practices committed *in, against* or *through* the company,[90] that is, internal reactions to *corporate crime.* These are the so-called internal investigations, whistleblowing channels and the application of penalties or disciplinary measures. It also involves the implementation of response/reaction protocols, meaning that the company must, in addition to detecting, investigating and sanctioning illicit acts, respond appropriately to the news of an offence, weighing, in each case, the need to report the facts to the authorities, repair damages or cooperate with public authorities.[91]

Beyond this, there must be proper institutionalisation in the execution of the programme; this means the designation of roles and responsibilities, that is, roles and responsibilities must be clearly defined so that, for each criminal risk, it is determined, through a system of delegations, which is responsible for the control/execution of a certain area of the programme.[92]

Finally, the improvement of the programmes implies their continuous evaluation, considering their routine need for updating, revision and, above all, a guarantee of effectiveness.[93]

Regarding the evaluation of the effectiveness of the programmes, William Laufer[94] mentions that, over 20 years ago, at a meeting at the United States Sentencing Commission with more than 500 participants, corporate experiences in developing effective *compliance* programmes were already being observed in contrast to what commonly became known as *compliance* comparative *window dressing*[95] or a 'cosmetic' use instrument—that is, the use of prevention programmes as mere defence mechanisms of the company, with little practical effect, appearing more as a mechanism of *marketing* and a merely formal paper programme (*paper programmes*).[96]

Even though at that time there were already warnings about the scepticism around self-regulation policies and about the need to take *compliance* programmes seriously, today, more than two decades later, difficulties are still encountered in determining the effectiveness of these.[97] This is because, as Laufer states, there is a

[89] Nieto Martín (2019a), p. 150.
[90] Rodrigues (2019), p. 58.
[91] Nieto Martín (2019a), p. 150.
[92] Nieto Martín (2019a), p. 150.
[93] Rodrigues (2019), p. 59.
[94] Laufer (2015), p. 57.
[95] Laufer (2015), p. 58.
[96] Nieto Martín (2013a), p. 144.
[97] Laufer (2015), p. 59.

compliance game (compliance game)[98] among some[99] interest groups, who utilise the industry of *compliance* and ethics to create an irresistibly appealing, yet superficial implementation, through which they seek to convince the *players* that there is a genuine commitment to corporate integrity,[100] but in reality, there is a lack of effective collaboration between these interest groups and *law enforcement* authorities.[101]

The ‘naive’ use of the understanding of regulated self-regulation, without any sophistication in the regulatory environment, gives rise to the *game* between regulators and the regulated, with the distancing between company, regulation and *enforcement,* causing ‘failures in the functional differentiation of law and absence of convergence between social control strategies and company regulation’.[102]

The most notable aspect of this game is that the *players* accommodate themselves in such a way that, inevitably, there is a regulatory balance in which ‘each player will gain a benefit (an advantage), without any player being excessively harmed so as to lose the game’.[103]

Given this scenario, there is slow progress towards definitive evidence regarding the effectiveness of *compliance*—that is, knowing whether the programmes really affect behaviour, decision-making or culture within the company—promoting a move towards effective self-regulation metrics.[104]

Therefore, it is essential to note some critical points that demand even greater attention in the establishment of *compliance programmes,* since determining their degree of effectiveness is one of the main problems of this tool. After all, how can one determine that a given *compliance* programme is effective in the prevention it proposes or is merely cosmetic? Any answer to this question requires a sufficiently scientific empirical basis to enable the identification of objective criteria that can measure such effectiveness. In other words, ‘special attention deserves the trend in evaluating *compliance* programmes based on the formation

[98] In more detail: ‘The *compliance* game is, indeed, a misnomer. It is, however, a subtle game, where institutional appearances are projected to maximise the legitimacy or an apparent legitimacy of each institutional player. The premise of this game of appearances is the desire for free and fair markets, without restrictions—as much as possible—imposed by burdensome regulation and, certainly, by criminal law’. (Our translation). Laufer (2015), p. 62.

[99] As the author warns, ‘it is clear that it would be naive and wrong to dismiss outright that some companies take compliance seriously and, as such, there are programmes, policies and cultures that positively influence employee behaviour’. (Our translation). Laufer (2015), p. 61.

[100] Laufer (2015), p. 59–60.

[101] Saad-Diniz (2018): 25–53, Feb.

[102] Saad-Diniz (2018), p. 28.

[103] Examples of this regulatory balance: the largest companies are spared from criminal prosecutions or, when they face charges, judicial agreements are offered, there are merely symbolic charges of high-profile defendants *high profile*, the rates of prosecution and conviction of economic crimes are stable etc. Laufer (2015), p. 60.

[104] Laufer (2015), p. 60.

of evidence (*evidence-based compliance*)',[105] whose metrics could provide a scientific foundation for the exercise of social control over corporations.[106]

Determining what an effective *compliance* programme is means establishing the general orientation of how and with what limits the criminal justice system expects companies to perform their preventive function. Undoubtedly, this is a criminal policy decision.[107] In this sense, it can also be said that there is a certain fundamentality in the evaluation of programmes for economic criminal law, as it is responsible for questioning the meaning of *compliance* guidelines in relation to standards of guilt, duties of care, normative elements of indeterminate criminal types or determination of criminal law.[108]

Regarding the criminal policy decision to be adopted by the justice system in establishing effectiveness metrics, one should consider which programme model is intended to be assumed as effective: (i) the one that directs compliance by implementing surveillance mechanisms or (ii) the one that considers that proper control should be done through the affirmation of a culture of corporate legality.[109]

The first model is guided by the adoption of surveillance control measures, such as access to emails, telephone call records, internet access, video surveillance, risk profile techniques or the 'criminal profile' of the employee, etc. Evidently, this way of assuming the evaluation of criminal risks in the company through surveillance techniques ensures greater control.[110]

The second model is guided by a value-based conception of *compliance* programmes; that is, it holds a structure of instruments guided by notably preventive values and is not intended for direct reaction through detection or indiscriminate *fishing* for offensive corporate behaviour, as is the case with the first model. It is noteworthy that reactive means are also used in the value-based model; however, they tend to be used ultimately in a context of legitimacy, similar to the distinction between preventive prosecution means and those used in the investigation of already committed crimes.[111]

Under these considerations, when referring to compliance systems with greater power of efficacy and credibility before the criminal justice system, the value-oriented proposal assumes prevalence, since, if the task is to determine the authenticity of the programmes through the realignment of corporate visions in the face of the routine cosmetic use,[112] one must assume as a measure of 'legitimacy' those programmes that, in fact, develop a culture of respect for legality and the company's ethical values.[113]

---

[105] Saad-Diniz (2019), p. 125.

[106] Saad-Diniz (2019), p. 125–126.

[107] Nieto Martín (2013b), p. 183.

[108] Sieber (2013), p. 301.

[109] Nieto Martín (2013b), p. 183.

[110] Nieto Martín (2013b), p. 184.

[111] Nieto Martín (2013b), p. 184.

[112] Laufer (2015), p. 65.

[113] In addition: 'Taking seriously that the strategy of compliance programmes is the promotion of internal values in line with respect for legality and fundamental rights should have consequences

After all, if legitimacy were granted to the surveillance model, the company would be transformed into a large-scale panopticon akin to *Big Brother*, which could impact fundamental rights to privacy, the secrecy of communications and the right to protection from harm.[114]

Therefore, it is necessary to assume that criminal law or *criminal compliance* will not, *per se*, favour the assumption of a value-oriented model. In other words, it must be recognised that the guarantee of effective *compliance* programmes comes, above all, from the influence of other branches, such as administrative law, business ethics and *standardisation* norms, which, ultimately, are clearly preventive measures and not surveillance.[115]

Indeed, reinforcing the legitimacy of *compliance* programmes means broadening the range of foundations to ensure greater credibility for the established structure, that is, bringing to the formulation of the programmes arguments other than the 'mere' criminal law,[116] that is, only as a way to seek exemption from responsibilities.

The reinforcement of legitimacy for the programmes goes through arguments of public law, labour law and CSR.[117] For the purposes of this work, direction will be given to the latter.

The issue of the legitimacy of the programmes has been especially discussed and developed within the scope of CSR and business ethics, with the due permeability of the corporation to the participation of the most varied sectors interested in corporate activity, which Nieto Martín notes as 'participation mechanisms' of the *stakeholders*.[118] Three paths of participation can be listed: (i) the possibility of being consulted, as independent advisors, in the elaboration of internal policies/norms through representatives of 'public interest', such as non-governmental organisations; (ii) the possibility of them effectively participating in the elaboration of internal norms that affect them; and (iii) providing information about the functioning of the *compliance* system, such as, for example, CSR or sustainability reports, with the commitment to provide truly useful data, both to interested groups and to public control.[119]

This theoretical framework for the pursuit of the effectiveness of the programmes, to escape from cosmetic use, is constituted by proposals such as *deliberative business ethics* or, also, *stakeholder democracy*. This fundamentally assumes the notions of

---

in the configuration of complaint channels or in the design of disciplinary sanction policies. The implementation of anonymous complaint channels [...] Whistleblowing, in summary, has a completely different meaning when it is inserted within a compliance programme aimed at promoting ethical values within the company. It becomes a demonstration of corporate civic action'. (Our translation). Laufer (2015), p. 65.

[114] Nieto Martín (2013b), p. 184.

[115] Nieto Martín (2013b), p. 184.

[116] Nieto Martín (2019a), p. 144–145.

[117] For a detailed explanation of the other arguments, see: Nieto Martín (2019a), p. 144–145.

[118] Nieto Martín (2019a), p. 146.

[119] Nieto Martín (2019a), p. 146–149.

CSR and good governance by adopting the model of legitimacy from deliberation, as proposed by Habermas. That is, 'it is about the transition from corporate governance to deliberative governance'.[120] On the other hand, it is about focusing the intervention (regulated self-regulation), whether administrative or criminal, more on the quality and efficacy of the internal self-regulation system and less, according to the traditional public control model, on verifying the compliance of the norm by its recipient.[121]

It is in this new and modern mode of *self-regulation,* characterised by less coercive and more dialogic intervention, that compliance programmes have a specific weight in modulating sanctions, 'insofar as a company that is concerned with establishing them and putting them into operation demonstrates a real willingness to prevent the commission of offences, notably crimes'.[122]

Under this framework, compliance programmes aim not only to promote a new ethical business culture but also, and above all, they assume the ultimate goal of preventing harm to legal goods, the violation of human rights[123] and the corresponding administrative, civil and, ultimately, criminal responsibility.[124]

For this reason, this new way of assuming normative commitments demands a new type of *law enforcement,* through which state action introduces a (new) level of law enforcement between the (violation of the) norm and the (application of) sanction or punishment. State action 'is therefore not so much directed at sanctioning or punishing as at "seeking the cooperation and participation of offenders, with the aim of correcting the defects that led to the violation of a norm,"'[125] in a clear restorative and victimological concern. In addition, 'in the context of business activity, this means that state intervention through *compliance* fulfils a socialising function'.[126]

When talking about a new type of *law enforcement,* we are not saying anything other than the (autonomous) criminal responsibility of legal entities, which will be the subject of the next and final topic.

4.2 The Criminal Liability of Legal Entities and the Prevention of Human Rights Violations

In the previous topics and sections, the current globalised context of economic activity was presented, in which fertile paths are provided for criminality in the business sphere. In a new criminal phenomenology practiced within business

---

[120] Nieto Martín (2019a), p. 186.

[121] Rodrigues (2020), p. 40.

[122] Rodrigues (2020), p. 40.

[123] Sánchez (2019), p. 90–91.

[124] Rodrigues (2020), p. 40.

[125] Rodrigues (2020), p. 40.

[126] Rodrigues (2020), p. 40.

organisations, with complex contexts and network structures, obstacles are raised to the identification, investigation and penalisation of criminal actions.[127]

Given the great influence currently exerted by economic power, criminological contributions point to undeniable insights into the evolution or reinterpretation of the classic definition, proposed by Sutherland, of *white-collar crime*, based on differential association. Indeed, 'it is noticed that many of the illicit practices were, in fact, reiterated eighty years later, with only the means of their perpetration being updated'.[128]

We currently speak of *respectable crime*, in which the company is presented as a 'focus of danger', as it would facilitate the commission of crimes due to the 'organised criminal irresponsibility' and the 'depersonalisation', which ensure the survival of the business organisation, since the individual perceives that he is just 'another cog in the machine'.[129]

In this new context, unravelled and clarified by criminology, the imperative need to sanction many economic behaviour was verified. In this sense, it is brought, especially to the criminal framework, the urgency to confront the aggression to criminal legal goods and human rights violations, which arises in the face of 'contexts of collective actions, in which "personal relations" are replaced by "anonymous and standardised behaviours" and that the risks are not only illusory [. . .] but are even greater [. . .]'.[130]

It is for no other reason than the compatibility and greater yield between criminal law and the already announced context of regulated self-regulation occurs, undoubtedly, with the criminal responsibility of collective persons, and the combination of regulated self-regulation with social responsibility is pointed out as the basis of this model of criminal responsibility.[131] This becomes more evident when analysing that, in public-private cooperation, the norm and its compliance no longer have a mere purpose of prohibiting conduct, but rather of encouraging learning processes associated with a non-differential standard, 'that is, tending towards strict normative compliance in the business sphere, thus presenting itself as an effective option for a model of social control of white-collar deviant behaviours'.[132]

The issue of criminal liability in the context of economic crimes takes on a crucial aspect in attributing this responsibility to collective entities in the face of *corporate crimes* and, above all, due to the prosperous connection with the field of regulated self-regulation. The central idea (or strategy) behind this theoretical

---

[127] Rodrigues (2020), p. 31.

[128] Sarcedo (2014), p. 88.

[129] Rodrigues (2020), p. 32.

[130] Rodrigues (2020), p. 33.

[131] Nieto (2008), p. 14.

[132] Sarcedo (2014), p. 95.

framework is that the introduction of corporate criminal liability aims to stimulate business self-regulation in order to establish effective methods to prevent, detect and punish a set of criminal behaviours.[133]

As already anticipated in the previous topic, regulatory compliance begins before compliance with criminal law, largely through the use of extrapenal frameworks and rules. Thus, the current task is to integrate this compliance system into Criminal Law and, more specifically, into the system of criminal liability—in a broad sense—of collective entities, with *compliance* programmes being key to deciding on the model of responsibility to be adopted.[134]

In view of the adoption of regulated self-regulation strategies, it is not overlooked that, in the search for the most appropriate treatment for political-criminal issues arising from corporate crime, much of the discussion relates to the relationship between *compliance* and the individual responsibility[135] of employees, managers and directors for the practice of or participation in *corporate crimes*. These, incidentally, deal with various theories of attribution of responsibility, from those that highlight the differentiation between author and participant to those that indicate joint criminal authorship, instigation-authorship and the control of the act,[136] in addition to debates about omissive crimes and the guarantor position of the businessman,[137] the crimes of duty infringement, the responsibility of the *compliance officer,* etc.[138]

However, without disregarding the essentiality of individual responsibility[139] in current times and still without wanting to exclude it from practical reality, a methodological cut is proposed in order to direct the present field of study towards the growing discussion about the legal entity itself—that is, the company—autonomously being criminally liable for crimes committed within its corporate structure.

In order to expose more clearly, it is pertinent to clarify the different models of corporate liability.[140]

---

[133] Nieto Martín (2020), p. 10.

[134] Nieto Martín (2019a), p. 181.

[135] Detailed in the Spanish system: Lascuraín (2018), p. 87–128.

[136] For specific details on individual liability in economic crimes see: Souza (2021).

[137] For more details: Silveira (2016).

[138] Souza (2015), p. 70 ff.

[139] Critically: 'While it is true that the obsessive search for better criteria of *individual accountability* has, however, shown low preventive yield, reduced to symbolic operations, it is also reasonable to assert that there is still much room for innovative theses regarding corporate criminal responsibility'. (Our translation). Saad-Diniz (2018), p. 31.

[140] It is important to highlight that the international trend of holding collective entities accountable does not necessarily impose criminal liability, it can be of an administrative or civil nature depending on the reality of each legal system. 'This seems to be true, as many countries have opted not for a criminal liability of the legal person, but for a liability of an administrative nature, more in terms of label than anything else'. (Our translation) Silveira and Saad-Diniz (2015), p. 82. Similarly, Leandro Sarcedo points out, Much more than the traditional quantitative criteria in defining what will integrate or not the criminal sphere and what will be relegated to the protection

4.2.1 *Frameworks for Corporate Criminal Liability in Brazil*

In the current context of preventing economic crime in the era of *compliance*, it is fundamental to observe the responsibility of the legal entity in its various aspects, including as a way to establish 'the variations on the *criminal compliance* in universes still in legislative formation, as seen in the Brazilian case'.[141]

It is pointed out, from the outset, that the proposal of criminal liability for collective entities, in general, is not exempt from criticism, especially for its supposed incompatibility with the principles of classic Criminal Law,[142] which is directed towards the protection of the individual and the legitimisation of the exceptional restrictions on their freedom.[143] Thus, collective imputation ends up encountering the difficulties of the classical framework in dealing with supra-individual criminality.[144]

However, in the current phase of 'modernisation' of the criminal branch, the increasing presence of Economic Criminal Law (see Item 3.1.2) points to a timely discussion about the direction of criminal liability of legal entities, especially when the main element connected to this reality is the company.[145] Not otherwise is the discussion justified by the international reality, which presents a necessary

---

administrative-sanctioning, it will be seen that the decisive, in reality, is the political-criminal decision to include a conduct in this or that branch of the legal system'. (Our translation). Sarcedo (2014), p. 96.

[141] Silveira and Saad-Diniz (2015), p. 79.

[142] 'There is strong resistance from the doctrine, both national and foreign, which remains faithful to traditional Criminal Law and, consequently, to the dogma *societas delinquere non potest*, according to the postulates of culpability and personality of penalties. The reasoning is in the absence, in the legal person, of the following elements: capacity for criminal action, capacity for culpability and capacity for punishment, indispensable elements for the configuration of subjective criminal responsibility'. (Our translation). Barrilari (2018), 121.

[143] Silveira and Saad-Diniz (2015), p. 79. For more details see: Shecaira (2020) *Criminologia*. 8th edn. Thomson Reuters, São Paulo, p. 502.

[144] Sarcedo (2014), p. 96.

[145] In this sense: 'Economic criminality itself, associated with the imputation pole called a company, cannot be ignored. If today the criminal liability of legal entities is a reality in many countries, the origins of the thought of repression to corporate crime are exactly in this period. A new type of crime emerges here: that of these labour aggregating centres—the company—and, with it, its study as a propositional and normative category within the legal-penal thought. The machine, a product of technique, is a potential element of dangers. The company, as an aggregation pole of interests, becomes, in some circumstances and within certain contexts, the centre of attention of the criminal scene. From this perspective, the company is not only an expression of a social reality, but also rationalises through a concept of manifest instrumental value. The company is, thus, one of the essential nodes of the way of being of the communities of the current post-industrial societies. It is not the place where or through which economic crime is triggered; it is, indeed, the *topos* from where economic crime can arise. Therefore, such a conception of things leads to the company being able to present itself as a true centre of criminal imputation'. (Our translation). Shecaira (2020), p. 502.

harmonisation of legal systems[146] as well as an understanding of the purpose of *compliance* in Criminal Law.[147]

Considering, therefore, the modern political-criminal strategies for the confrontation of economic crime, the criminal liability of the legal entity becomes a reinforcement of traditional techniques of formal social control over criminal conduct of an economic nature,[148] so that, in the current scenario, the maxim axiom *societas delinquere non potest*, which governed the matter until the mid-twentieth century,[149] appears somewhat unreasonable. '*Societas delinquere non potest is clearly on its way out*'.[150]

A relevant aspect to be noted concerns the political-criminal choice in attributing infractions to companies, that is, the decision to act through administrative law or economic criminal law, being certain that the administrative sanctioning activity has developed to the point of understanding that it is part of a generic, but unified, *ius puniendi* of the state.[151] In any case, 'it is necessary to verify which models of attribution reveal greater capacity to assign operational effectiveness to the criminal liability of the legal entity'[152] and—it is noted—to converge positively in the effectiveness of *compliance* programmes.

The debate about these different approaches to confront the illegal actions of legal entities proves to be of enormous value in the Brazilian reality, which, in recent years, points to the institution of administrative responsibility for collective entities, notably through the approval of Federal Law No. 12.846/2013, the already mentioned Anti-Corruption Law or Clean Company Law. As already mentioned (see Item 3.1.1), this legislation provides for the objective liability of legal entities for the practice of illegal acts that affront the national or foreign administration.

There is a thin dividing line between administrative infraction and economic crime; what differentiates them, in truth, is a legislative option of political-criminal

---

146 'The criminal liability of legal entities is largely the result of the process of harmonisation of criminal law that we have been witnessing in the last two decades. During this period, the legislative landscape has changed with enormous speed due to the fact that the criminal liability of legal entities forms part of the hard core of international criminal policy, coming from the EU, OECD, United Nations, the Council of Europe or the OAS'. (Our translation). Nieto Martín and Moreno (2019), pp. 635–636.

147 Silveira and Saad-Diniz (2015), p. 80.

148 Sarcedo (2014), p. 96.

149 Souza (2021).

150 Brodowski et al. (eds) (2014) *Regulating Corporate Criminal Liability*. Springer, New York, p. 1.

151 In addition: 'Within this current understanding about the unitary character of the *ius puniendi* of the state, the tendency is that the rules and guarantees of the sanctioning administrative law, as a punitive order, are no longer oriented by the principles of administrative law, but rather of criminal law. Thus, the formulation and application of sanctioning administrative law are governed by principles and rules, such as: a) legality and its consequent prohibition of legal retroactivity; b) culpability [...]; c) mechanisms of exclusion of injustice and culpability, for example, legitimate defence and state of necessity; d) criteria for assessing authorship and participation'. (Our translation). Sarcedo (2014), p. 100.

152 Sarcedo (2014), p. 96.

content—content that is eminently qualitative in relation to the treatment given to the fact. Thus, in practice, criminal law and sanctioning administrative law end up overlapping, without being able to verify the differentiation between the purposes of the penalty and the administrative sanction.[153]

In the midst of criminal law and sanctioning administrative law, as major branches of the *ius puniendi*, the liability of the legal entity for crimes committed within it—whether for its benefit or for the individuals involved—is set as a real alternative of criminal policy. This appears as a way of 'providing a coherent and concrete response to the need to establish new parameters for confronting corporate crime',[154] especially when considering the deficit of administrative responsibility for the transfer of responsibility to the legal entity for a criminal action of the physical person, whether by commission or omission. In this sense, it is pointed out as difficult to attribute responsibility to the company in an objective way, 'when the action or omission of the agent who has transferred the responsibility to the company is a criminally relevant action or omission, that is, depends on intent or fault'.[155]

Despite this, and although there is constitutional permission—as will be seen following this—legitimising the criminal liability of legal entities in acts of corruption and general corporate crimes, it is possible to observe that the legislator sought to circumvent the Brazilian legal-penal doctrinal environment resistant to the adoption of this type of responsibility and ended up basing corporate accountability on the *ius puniendi* arising from the punitive administrative[156] system.

There are several criticisms regarding the adoption of administrative responsibility, including, in particular, the legal irrelevance given to the efforts made by companies to structure and implement, in practice, good corporate governance practices and *compliance*. These efforts are relegated solely to possible mitigators of the penalty at the time of its application, but never as a potential element for excluding imputation, given the objective nature of the responsibility model adopted.[157] In this sense, it 'seems unreasonable to argue that clause VIII of art. 7 of Law n. 12.846/2013 constitutes a "stimulus structure" for the implementation of *compliance programmes* by companies'.[158]

Hence, the argument that combating corruption requires the CLLE, 'allied to the provision of a preventive system, aimed at acting on two lines: in advance, in the *ante factum* of the crime, and subsequently, as the establishment of consequences

[153] There are many debates around the topic, such as the need to expand constitutional guarantees to the sanctioning administrator, lack of specific delimitation of the legal goods protected by the sanctioning administrative law, application of *ne bis in idem*, among others. For more details on the discussions see: Sarcedo (2014), p. 100 ff.

[154] Barrilari (2018), p. 118.

[155] Barrilari (2018), p. 216.

[156] Sarcedo (2014), p. 168.

[157] Sarcedo (2014), p. 168.

[158] Sarcedo (2014), p. 169.

for the *post delictum*'.[159] This means that a model of accountability is demanded, one that truly encourages the investment of the high costs involved in implementing preventive programmes.

In this way, the assumption of the CLLE, 'unlinked from the physical person, that is, by the creation of a system of culpability of its own', is relevant because it considers 'the efforts of the legal entity in implementing an efficient mechanism for crime prevention'. This difference, although subtle, is the balance that can give effectiveness and efficiency to prevention programmes and *compliance* programmes.[160]

The models of CLLE are classified based on the relationships established between individual responsibility and corporate responsibility, that is, from the way these responsibilities communicate. Generally, the basis of the models occurs in two ways: through heteroresponsibility and self-responsibility.[161]

In this sense, the current objective of the discussion relates, above all, to the identification of the model most compatible with the reality in which it is found, as well as to the verification of a smaller dogmatic deficit in holding the legal entity responsible by identifying the physical person responsible for the illicit (hetero-responsibility), or if it is possible to identify a sufficient degree of independence to hold the legal entity responsible *per se,* unlinked from the physical person who relates to it (self-responsibility).[162]

In the heteroresponsibility or heteronomous model, also known as the vicarious model, by transfer or by ricochet,[163] the responsibility for the conduct carried out by an administrator or employee, in the exercise of their activity and with the intention of benefiting the legal entity, is transferred to the collective entity.[164] Thus, for this model, the assignment of responsibility requires three elements or conditions: (i) a corporate employee as the active agent of the infraction; (ii) an infraction committed due to the official functions assigned to the agent; (iii) and the objective of obtaining some type of advantage or benefit for the company.[165]

There are several criticisms of this model:[166] (i) the possible unconstitutionality due to the violation of the principle of responsibility for one's own act; (ii) the attractive suggestion of this regime for the adoption of mechanisms to shift or slide the risk of the crime from the administrators to the subordinates; (iii) and also, the effect of discouraging the implementation of effective *compliance* programmes, that is, the absence of reward for the efforts adopted by the offender in an attempt

[159] Barrilari (2018), p. 223.

[160] Barrilari (2018), p. 223.

[161] Barrilari (2018), p. 122.

[162] Barrilari (2018), p. 117.

[163] Barrilari (2018), p. 122.

[164] Given this characteristic, this model can be termed as responsibility by attribution. Silva Sánchez (2008), p. 130.

[165] Nieto Martín (2019a), p. 81.

[166] As presented by Nieto Martín (2019a), p. 82.

to comply with the law.[167] In this last aspect, the company, 'even if it develops or implements internal controls or measures aimed at preventing or identifying illicit acts, this will not have effects on the attribution of responsibility'.[168]

Beyond these criticisms, Silva Sánchez[169] similarly points out three problems inherent to this model. The first relates to the tendency to hold the person at the lower level in the company's hierarchical structure accountable. The second refers to cases where no individual is identified as the author of the act to be attributed to the corporate entity.[170] And the third highlights the case of the unimpressibility of the individual's action, whose responsibility will be transferred to the legal entity.

The second of these problems stands out, drawing attention to what the author calls situations of 'organised irresponsibility', in which the inherent difficulty of establishing criminal responsibility within the broad business complex emerges. Added to this difficulty is the preventive insufficiency of individual responsibility, 'insofar as, even in cases where it is possible to identify the natural person [...] it would fall short of what is necessary to face the risks of corporate crime'.[171] It is also pointed out that there is a preventive insufficiency of non-penal forms of collective responsibility, 'as administrative sanctions would not be adequate for most corporate offences'.[172]

Complementing these ideas, Leandro Sarcedo[173] points out the difficulties faced in the use of classic criminal imputation intended for individuals in corporate crime: '(1) either the way the criminal environment operates is not known (the causal link), (2) or the perpetrator of the damage is not known (delimitation of authorship), (3) or, finally, the victims are not identified (mass victimisation)'.

The author also mentions the absence of differentiation in this model in relation to that provided by the sanctioning administration, so that neither allows for the assessment of the company's own culpability, both being based on the transfer of individual responsibility to the collective, which, in practice, evidently means objective liability.[174]

---

[167] In addition: 'If administrative law The sanctioning body does not recognise the efforts that the company has made to comply with the legal system, and treats companies that have been diligent and those that have neglected preventive aspects equally. It is normal for the former to refuse to allocate resources for the improvement of *compliance*'. Nieto Martín (2019a), p. 83.

[168] Barrilari (2018), p. 123.

[169] Silva Sánchez (2008), p. 130.

[170] Another criticism related to this aspect is highlighted: 'It is emphasised how the model of hetero-responsibility fails especially in large companies, where it is more difficult, due to complexity, to find an individual responsible. Conditioning the company's liability to the demonstration that a manager, in relation to a specific criminal act and a subordinate, violated his supervision duties, *would mean consecrating a model of corporate responsibility that would benefit large companies and harm smaller ones*, since in these it is much easier to locate the responsibility or the specific lack of surveillance of a manager or director'. (emphasis added). (Our translation). Rodrigues (2020), p. 35.

[171] Souza (2021), p. 155.

[172] Souza (2021), p. 155–156.

[173] Sarcedo (2014), p. 136.

[174] Sarcedo (2014), p. 136.

As for the model of self-responsibility, the possibility is rooted in the company being liable, by itself and based on its own culpability, for criminal responsibility in the face of an organisational defect or the so-called *culpability due to organisational defect.*[175] That is, the company can be held accountable if it allows, in its collective decision-making and in its careless actions, its members—administrators, managers or employees—to commit crimes in its favour, or, still, because, through its decisions, it opted for an action directed at the practice of crimes.[176]

In summary, the criminal responsibility of the company *qua tale* is based on the understanding of the idea of organisational defect or the company's own culpability,[177] which means to say that the corporation did not adequately prevent the practice of illicit acts by those subjects that compose it. Or still, as Anabela Rodrigues aptly points out,[178] 'the company did not care enough to counteract the criminogenic effect that the benefits that its administrators, managers and employees derive from favouring the company through the practice of crimes [. . .]'.

In this model, it is understood that the culpability of the corporate entity represents more than the accumulation of the culpabilities of the natural persons that compose it, which does not mean to say that corporate responsibility excludes these, being able to implement the idea of 'collective culpability (or group or corporate) alongside traditional individual culpability. Under no aspect, are they incompatible'.[179]

This reality of self-responsibility ends up requiring that corporations adopt preventive models of *compliance* intended to prevent illicit activities within their corporate structure, related to the activity in which they are involved. When this idea is put in a cross-cutting manner, the lack of implementation of these normative instruments within the organisation 'actually results in the factual situation that dogmatics calls *organisational defect*, that is, the corporate attitude of "not having adopted all reasonable and indispensable organisational measures to prevent this or that crime"'.[180]

A third way is the mixed models of responsibility, which combine, to some extent, both previous models, being called mixed models of imputation. In truth, each model will depend on the legal system in which it is inserted; however, it can be said that, as a rule, they start from the vicarious model or heteroresponsibility as a way to transfer to the company the responsibility for a certain fact committed by a corporate agent for its benefit, but they assume the corporate culpability of self-responsibility as a way to assess whether the preventive measures serve as

[175] Nieto Martín (2013b), p. 181.

[176] Rodrigues (2020), p. 34.

[177] Nieto Martín (2019a), p. 83.

[178] Rodrigues (2020), p. 35.

[179] Sarcedo (2014), p. 133.

[180] Sarcedo (2014), p. 134.

possible elements of modulation of the penalty to be applied or even the acquittal of the collective entity.[181]

Among all these models, it is opportune to highlight the Brazilian reality regarding the criminal responsibility of the legal entity.

In a synthetic way, it is underlined that the assumption of the institute by the Federal Constitution of 1988, through its Art. 225, paragraph 3, enshrines corporate responsibility in relation to infractions against the environment, stating that 'conducts and activities harmful to the environment will subject the offenders, individuals or legal entities, to criminal and administrative sanctions, regardless of the obligation to repair the damages caused'. This provision is regulated by the Environmental Crimes Law (Law No. 9.605/98).

Also, it is worth noting the possibility brought by Art. 173, paragraph 5, of the Constitution, which provides for the responsibility of the legal entity, without prejudice to the individual responsibility of its directors, subjecting them to punishments compatible with their nature for acts committed against the economic and financial order and against the popular economy. This provision still lacks its own regulation, and little progress has been made in its implementation.[182]

For Saad-Diniz, over the three decades since the constitutional adoption of the institute, at least five historical moments have been identified: (i) rejection by the doctrine; (ii) counter-majoritarian tendencies; (iii) reception in jurisprudential interpretation; (iv) reinforcement through the introduction of *compliance* programmes in Brazil; and (v) indeterminacy of the concept and the search for new regulatory parameters.[183]

Regarding the first moments, it can be said, in general, that despite certain digressions and disagreements regarding the admission of criminal responsibility of the legal entity, the understanding was consolidated that the Constitution enshrined the criminal imputability of the legal entity, assuming jurisprudentially the conception of the so-called 'system of double imputation', that is, the CLLE would depend on the identification of the individual conduct practiced.[184]

---

[181] In addition: 'In the words of Adán NIETO MARTÍN, with mixed models, the aim is to obtain the best of each model. From one perspective, the ease and legal certainty resulting from the model of hetero-responsibility, with its alleged ability to transfer to the company, through the application of the pertinent sanction, the totality of the social costs resulting from the criminal action. On the other hand, the stimulus to organisational improvements in companies, including with mechanisms of incentive to denunciations and reparations for facts that have already occurred or are in progress, as they result in the possibility of acquittal or mitigation of the penalty'. (Our translation). Sarcedo (2014), p. 138.

[182] Shecaira and Sarcedo (2014), p. 690.

[183] Saad-Diniz (2018), 988:42.

[184] According to Law No. 9.605/98, 'the responsibility of the corporation does not exclude that of the individual, author, co-author, participant in the same fact. In this context, it is initially revealed that the imputation of the criminal responsibility of the corporation depends on the identification of the conduct carried out by the legal or contractual representative, or its collegiate body'. Barrilari (2018), p. 127–128.

Leandro Sarcedo[185] aptly provides insights about the measurable difficulties of this interpretation of double imputation, mentioning the confusion in the necessary concurrence of agents of a material nature with the procedural necessity of linking physical agents to the legal entity in the description of the criminal fact. According to the author, accepting that every fact attributable to a legal entity has been necessarily committed by a physical person means requiring a kind of necessary concurrence of agents between natural individuals and the collective entity.[186]

The debate took a new turn when the First Chamber of the Superior Federal Court, in RE 548.181/PR, on August 6, 2013, through the vote of the rapporteur, Minister Rosa Weber,[187] innovated the jurisprudence by a majority of three favourable votes and changed the system of double imputation for environmental crimes, notably for the reasons and conclusions argued in the leading vote.

Thus, in many situations, the search for criminal responsibility of the legal entity, without the same illicit fact having been attributed to a precisely identified physical person, may result from an almost practical impossibility of proving human responsibility within the corporation due to horizontal and vertical division of assignments; or from a recognised softening of individual faults in the face of the structural and organic complexity of the functioning and decisions of the moral entity, leading to a softening of personal responsibilities to the point where the collaboration of each physical person becomes diluted in the imputation process. For these reasons, the 1988 Federal Constitution (Art. 225, § 3º) allows for the

---

[185] Sarcedo (2014), p. 150–151.

[186] Sarcedo (2014), p. 150–151.

[187] 'EXTRAORDINARY APPEAL. CRIMINAL LAW. ENVIRONMENTAL CRIME. CORPORATE CRIMINAL RESPONSIBILITY. CONDITIONING OF THE CRIMINAL ACTION TO THE IDENTIFICATION AND CONCURRENT PERSECUTION OF THE INDIVIDUAL THAT IS NOT SUPPORTED BY THE CONSTITUTION OF THE REPUBLIC. 1. Article 225, § 3º, of the Federal Constitution does not condition the criminal liability of the corporation for environmental crimes to the simultaneous criminal prosecution of the individual allegedly responsible within the company. The norm The constitution does not impose the necessary dual imputation. 2. Today's complex corporate organisations are characterised by decentralisation and distribution of duties and responsibilities, with the inherent difficulties of attributing the unlawful act to a specific individual. 3. *To condition the application of art. 225, §3º, of the Political Charter to a concrete imputation also to a physical person implies an undue restriction of the constitutional norm, expressing the intention of the original constituent not only to expand the scope of criminal sanctions, but also to prevent impunity for environmental crimes in the face of immense difficulties in individualising those responsible within corporations, as well as reinforcing the protection of the environmental legal good.* 4. The identification of the sectors and internal agents of the company responsible for the production of the unlawful act is relevant and should be sought in the specific case as a way to clarify whether these individuals or bodies acted or deliberated in the regular exercise of their internal duties to the society, and also to verify whether the action was in the interest or benefit of the collective entity. *Such clarification, relevant for the purpose of attributing a certain crime to a legal entity, does not, however, confuse with subordinating the liability of the legal entity to the joint and cumulative liability of the physical persons involved. On not rare occasions, the internal responsibilities for the fact will be diluted or partialised in such a way that they will not allow the imputation of individual criminal responsibility.* 5. Extraordinary Appeal partially known and, in the known part, provided'. (emphasis added). Brazil. Supremo Tribunal Federal (2013) Extraordinary Appeal 548.181. Rapporteur Min. Rosa Weber. 6 Aug 2013.

punishment of a legal entity without necessarily attributing the same criminal act to an individual, provided it is demonstrated that the offence resulted from decisions or actions committed by individuals or bodies linked to the company, in the regular exercise of their internal duties to society, as behaviours accepted by the legal entity, pertaining to its ordinary social operation; and even if such operation was carried out in the interest or for the benefit of the collective entity.

Given all the above, I partially acknowledge the Extraordinary Appeal and, in the acknowledged part, I grant it to recognise the possibility that the indictment for environmental crime against the legal entity does not necessarily encompass the criminal attribution of the fact also to the individual, and order the regular processing of the criminal action against Petrobras[188] (our emphasis).[189]

Although the understanding does not imply complete consensus for overcoming double imputation, the analysis undertaken by the leading vote can, according to Sarcedo, denote some criteria for penal attribution to the legal entity: (i) ascertain whether the offence committed resulted from the regular process of internal deliberation of the corporation; (ii) ascertain whether there was knowledge, acceptance or inertia of the internal bodies regarding the illicit act; (iii) examine whether the criminal conduct was in line with the company's standards and objectives and aimed to achieve its social objectives, having been carried out in its name; and (iv) demonstrate whether the act was committed in the interest or benefit of the corporation.[190]

From these criteria, as argued by the leading vote, the author highlights that it is possible to anticipate an approximation of the 'discussion of the idea of *organisational defect* in business'[191] with a possible tendency to admit the autonomous imputation of crime to legal entities. In this way, 'it is necessary to regulate organisational duties, compliance and prevention of crimes minimally required of legal entities [. . .]'.[192]

Concluding on the subject, Artur Gueiros Souza points out that the basis of this change in orientation rested on the fact that Art. 225, §3º, of the 1988 Federal Constitution did not, in fact, impose double imputation. Moreover, the author notes that 'complex corporate organisations of today are characterised by decentralisation

---

[188] Brazil. Supremo Tribunal Federal (2013) *Extraordinary Appeal 548.181*. Rapporteur Min. Rosa Weber. 6 Aug 2013.

[189] It is important to note that the Superior Court of Justice has similarly begun to consider the unnecessary dual imputation, so that the RPPJ for environmental crimes can occur regardless of the concurrent liability of the physical person who committed the conduct, as can be seen in some rulings whose summaries collide 'environmental crimes—criminal liability of the legal entity—is not conditioned to the simultaneous criminal prosecution of the physical person'. Brazil. Superior Court of Justice (6th Chamber) (2018) Regimental Appeal in Writ of Mandamus 48.851/PA. Rapporteur Min. Nefi Cordeiro. 20 February; Brazil. Superior Court of Justice (6th Chamber) (2015) Appeal in Habeas Corpus 48.172/PA. Rapporteur Min. Sebastião Reis Júnior. 20 October; Brazil. Superior Court of Justice (5th Chamber) (2015) *Appeal in Writ of Mandamus 39.173/ BA*. Rapporteur Min. Reynaldo Soares da Fonseca. 6 August.

[190] Sarcedo (2014), p. 155.

[191] Sarcedo (2014), p. 155.

[192] Sarcedo (2014), p. 155.

and distribution of duties and responsibilities, inherent to this reality are the difficulties in attributing the illicit act to a specific person'.[193]

The debate gained new momentum with the promotion of *compliance* programmes and the profusion of new theses about the political-criminal reorientation and the possibilities of regulated self-regulation, opening the fifth moment of indeterminacy of the concept in which new regulatory parameters are sought.[194] This is because only from a clear and secure system, with known provisions of duties and obligations, will the *compliance programmes* have their role enhanced. In the absence of benchmarks of corporate culpability, companies that invest in risk prevention and those that ignore such a need are equated on the same level, 'causing, from another aspect, the loss of the effectiveness intended by the political-criminal tool of attributing criminal responsibility to legal entities'.[195]

In this panorama brought about by the jurisprudential turn, it can be said that there has been, in Brazil, an abandonment of the model of heteroresponsibility to approach the model of self-responsibility or, at least, a Brazilian hybrid model.[196]

Finally, a brief mention must be made of the Draft Penal Code (PLS 236) under consideration in the Federal Senate, which provides, in its Art. 41, the responsibility of legal entities for acts against the environment, but also for those set forth in Art. 173, paragraph 5, of the Federal Constitution. See:

Art. 41. Private legal entities shall be criminally liable for acts committed against public administration, economic order, the financial system and the environment, in cases where the infraction is committed by decision of their legal or contractual representative, or their collegiate body, in the interest or benefit of the entity.

§1 The liability of legal entities does not exclude that of individuals, authors, co-authors or participants in the same act, nor is it dependent on their accountability.

§2 The dissolution of the legal entity or its acquittal does not exclude the liability of the individual.

§3 Anyone who, in any way, contributes to the commission of the crimes referred to in this article incurs the penalties imposed on them to the extent of their culpability, as well as the director, the administrator, the member of the board and of the technical body, the auditor, the manager, the representative or agent of the legal entity who, knowing of the criminal conduct of another, fails to prevent its practice when they could act to prevent it.[197]

Although the new legislative provisions are commendable, particularly as they follow international trends, Leandro Sarcedo and Sérgio Salomão Shecaira not only point out the need for greater technical accuracy but also note the already outdated dogmatic and criminal-political aspects, especially in light of compliance programmes

---

193 Souza (2021), p. 173.

194 Saad-Diniz (2018), p. 44.

195 Sarcedo (2014), p. 156.

196 Souza (2021), p. 173.

197 Brazil. Federal Senate (2012) *Senate Bill No. 236, of 2012*. Preliminary Draft of the Penal Code. Special Secretariat for Editing and Publications, Brasília.

and corporate risk management forming a concept of culpability specific to collective entities, 'which includes not only the assessment of the harmful result, but also any organisational defect of the company, which would serve as a legitimising prerequisite for the penalty and also as a tool to contain state punitive power.[198]

4.2.2 *Corporate Criminal Self-Liability and Compliance Strategies in Preventing Human Rights Violations*

Although the depth of the topic and the essential aspects to be considered are not unknown, by assuming a certain model of attributing responsibility to the legal entity as preferable, it has been discussed so far that the criminal self-liability of collective entities appears as a possible institute to converge with the need for law enforcement in promoting preventive mechanisms (compliance) to human rights violations (see Chap. 2) beyond the prevention of corporate crime.

Eduardo Saad-Diniz,[199] when concluding about the performance of the criminal justice system in relation to the punishment of companies in Brazil over the last thirty years, points out that 'there are reasonable arguments that allow us to affirm that the regulation of socially harmful corporate behaviour is somewhat adrift in Brazil'. This is because it is perceived that the lack of sophistication in business regulation or law enforcement leads to a less collaborative attitude from companies and greater ostentation and selectivity in the operations of moralising business and political customs.[200]

Furthermore, the author highlights the priority coercion of individual aspects, so that to companies, the cooperative orientation loses sense, as well as the idea that 'the absence of regulatory paradox with the certainty of punishment of legal entities, leads to abstract modellings of self-regulation for a deleterious state of structural decoupling'.[201]

In this scenario, and paying attention to the moral indignation[202] against the criminal acts committed by large corporations and the failure of the criminal justice system to punish white-collar crimes and corporate crimes—often based on the frequent rhetoric of the regulatory game—[203] it becomes imperative to discuss the

---

[198] Shecaira and Sarcedo (2014), p. 704–705.

[199] Saad-Diniz (2018) Brazil vs. Goliath. *Law Rev* 988. p. 52.

[200] Saad-Diniz (2018), p. 52.

[201] Saad-Diniz (2018), p. 52.

[202] Laufer (2014), p. 19–21.

[203] 'When we think about the evils perpetrated by drug cartels and terrorist organisations, who thinks about the facilitating role of HSBC? There is no perennial if not perpetual fear of corporate deviance touching and compromising our lives. Quite simply, our sense of being wronged by corporations and their agents does not engender a brand of moral outrage, indignation, and fear adequate to support a fair, equitable, and proportional regime of corporate criminal justice'. Laufer (2014), p. 19–21.

possibility of a specific action by the legal entity to justify the formulation of a culpability specific to the company, in order to allow its autonomous accountability for its socially harmful behaviours, as already announced in the previous topic regarding the model of self-liability.

In addition, an autonomous model of corporate criminal liability becomes preferable, given the effectiveness of the preventive measures adopted by companies according to this model, as the combination of this liability with self-regulation appears as a 'win-win' solution, encouraging companies to develop their activity without committing illegal acts, notably criminal ones.[204]

It is worth noting here the necessary methodological scope of this work, which, although it does not have the margin to discuss the topic in an appropriate manner, does not overlook its fundamental importance. This is relevant when discussing the autonomous responsibility of the company, as it is grounded in the understanding and formulation of a unique method of attributing and assigning blame to companies, on which there is no doctrinal consensus.[205] There are several difficulties in formulating the unique culpability of the personalised collective entity,[206] so only brief mentions of the subject will be made.

By establishing a model of attribution to the company that places responsibility for its own actions, it seems reasonable to conclude that *compliance* programmes are a key piece in deterring responsibility for an organisational defect or the so-called 'culpability due to organisational defect',[207] just as they are tools for excluding attribution when their obligations have been satisfactorily fulfilled.[208] Clearly, it is necessary for the concept of organisational defect to be defined, with clear and precise legal requirements, outlining the minimum and non-reducible duties that a company must observe in the conduct of its social activity.[209]

Furthermore, the establishment of the relationship between the crime committed and the possible failure in the *compliance* programme is pointed out as relevant, with some arguing that the non-implementation or defective implementation of a compliance programme implies reckless favouritism (complicity) in the crime committed by the individual author, in such a way that it is considered useful to

---

[204] Rodrigues (2020), pp. 36–37.

[205] Silva Sánchez (2008) The ideological evolution. *Crim Law Criminol* 29(86–87):129–148.

[206] Silva Sánchez (2008), p. 129–148.

[207] Nieto Martín (2013b), p. 181.

[208] Sarcedo (2014). Put another way: 'the company did not exercise due control so that crimes were not committed in its favour from within its ranks. Or even more emphatically: the company did not care enough to counteract *the criminogenic effect that the benefits for its administrators, directors and employees entail when favouring the company in a market like the current one, highly competitive'. (emphasis added). RODRIGUES. A. (2019), p. 66.*

[209] Also, in addition: 'the importance of this deepening arises not only from the necessary definition of criteria and parameters for measuring corporate culpability resulting from organisational failure, but also as a system of guarantees, as it is the right of economic activity to know what is required of it and what can be demanded by the penal instance'. (Our translation). Sarcedo (2014), p. 245.

attribute the fact to the business through the theory of objective attribution. The non-adoption or defective adoption of the programme would represent an unauthorised risk, which would be realised in the result (the commission of the crime by the individual author). Some also argue that the organisational defect would be equivalent to a *Vorverschulden*[210] of the company.[211]

Nieto Martín announces that, although these approaches may demonstrate some correct intuition, they do not allow for the methodologically appropriate capture of the relationship between the organisational defect and the crime committed by the individual author, as the infraction of the legal entity cannot be reduced to mere reckless participation in the crime committed by the physical person. In truth, when talking about attributing criminal responsibility to the collective entity, what is truly important is—simply—the severity of the organisational defect,[212] which is assessable by a structure different from that present in individual responsibility.[213]

Unlike the temporal structure of individual responsibility, directed at the exact moment of the commission of the offence, in the responsibility of the collective entity, what matters is a longer time sequence, so as to encompass circumstances and moments before and after the criminal act.[214]

The company's fault is a permanent management defect, so the crime committed by a single physical person should not be considered as the ultimate result of an organisational defect.[215] To ascertain this, what must be demonstrated, in fact, is that the legal entity, in a continuous manner, did not adopt effective measures to prevent criminal acts of the kind verified and in the form concretely manifested.[216] This involves carrying out what Nieto Martín points out as the 'abstract-concrete adequacy test', to be conducted in a judgement of suitability regarding the compliance programme.[217]

When carrying out the aforementioned 'test' to ascertain the effectiveness of the programme, especially in judicial analysis of the possible responsibility of the collective entity, it should be examined from two perspectives: firstly, the general aspects of the programme are analysed and secondly, the effectiveness of the programme in the specific event that occurred is investigated.[218]

In the first part, the abstract effectiveness of the compliance programme and its implementation is examined as a guide to verifying whether, indeed, serious efforts

---

[210] Free translation from German: prior failure or defect.

[211] Nieto Martín (2013b), p. 187.

[212] Nieto Martín (2013b), p. 188.

[213] Nieto Martín (2013b), p. 189.

[214] Nieto Martín (2013b), p. 189. A certain preventive ideology 'that incorporates the "logic of anticipation" of the punishability of conduct already within the company itself'. Saad-Diniz (2015), p. 82.

[215] Nieto Martín (2013b), p. 189.

[216] Nieto Martín (2013b), p. 189.

[217] Nieto Martín (2013b), p. 189.

[218] Nieto Martín (2013b), p. 190.

are made by the company's management (*top-down*) to create a culture of legality and establish appropriate controls. The second part examines, based on the specific criminal case, the existence of preventive measures for similar events to those that occurred, as well as seeks to determine why they failed in the specific case.[219]

The two parts are sequential, so if the company does not pass the first part of the test, it indicates a very high degree of organisational fault or defect, with failures in the basic structure of the compliance system and in the implementation of a culture of legality by senior management. In this circumstance, there is no reason to discuss or investigate specific preventive measures, as the 'basic' is a condition for the effectiveness of the 'specific'.[220]

On the other hand, not 'passing' or not overcoming the second phase of the test—the analysis of the concrete situation—does not mean that there is a total disregard for the culture of compliance. On the contrary, it only indicates that there was a specific failure in the execution of the programme in a particular aspect.[221] In the words of Nieto Martín, the fact that the programme has 'failed punctually, despite its good operation in general and continuously, indicates a lesser degree of organisational defect that should be taken into account in the determination of the sanction'.[222]

Two circumstances emerge from this interpretative spectrum pointed out by the Spanish author, especially from the second phase of the 'test': (i) the concretisation of the specific test will be greater the more a standardisation and development of specific measures for the prevention of certain crimes and their different forms of manifestation are achieved; (ii) within the limits brought by this test, it can be noted that the programme is effective when the criminal agent has to evade several controls and infringe the company's normative regulations.[223]

From these circumstances, and assuming the defect of the organisation as a crucial pillar of corporate self-responsibility, it is possible to infer some reflections on to what extent one can think of the interaction between CLLE, *criminal compliance* and prevention of human rights violations, especially when it is intended to have in view, in addition to the greater effectiveness of self-regulation programmes, the guarantee of a more functional relationship between these and state regulatory and social control strategies.

The step of assuming the possibility of collective entities being held accountable for themselves, autonomously, enhances the aspirations of promoting corporate self-regulation, as this 'new type' of *law enforcement* favours the cooperative action of private entities in correcting the defects[224] that may have led to criminal infractions and human rights violations by the company, with a view to preventing not only new occurrences but also criminal liability itself.

---

[219] Nieto Martín (2013b), p. 190.

[220] Nieto Martín (2013b), p. 190.

[221] Nieto Martín (2013b), p. 190.

[222] Nieto Martín (2013b), p. 191.

[223] Nieto Martín (2013b), p. 190.

[224] Rodrigues (2020), p. 40.

According to Saad-Diniz, the analysis of the limits imposed on the company, between coercion and cooperation, 'can offer to the programmes of *compliance* the domains of ethical behaviour and the evaluation of maturity of controls, if they point to obsession [. . .] or if they favour the creation of conditions for prosocial behaviour'.[225] This is because, as the author concludes, social control 'encourages cooperative behaviour to the extent that it reviews its coercive strategies, conferring on the private sector the responsibility for controlling corporate crime'.[226]

For the best use of this environment of *self-regulation*, it must be assumed by criminal policy a posture oriented to the value conception of *compliance* programmes,[227] that is, to consider them as part of the political-criminal strategy of social control. Indeed, this approach reaches actions where criminal law does not extend and can even go beyond what the law provides, affirming the character of *ultima ratio* of criminal law.[228]

Assuming compliance programmes as a legitimate source of prevention requires, as already seen, investment in ensuring that they have greater effectiveness and credibility before the criminal justice system.[229] This can only be achieved through the legitimacy criteria set by criminal policy itself, which must take into account, for greater efficiency, the need for corporate permeability to interests arising from social responsibility and business ethics.[230]

In other words, the concern of corporations with topics of *business ethics*, and especially with the inclusion and participation of interested groups (*stakeholders*), is what elevates the level of *compliance* programmes from mere instruments of liability prevention to true social mechanisms for the protection and promotion of human rights.[231]

It is necessary to highlight that the propositions to elevate corporate culture to a new level of mentality are notably susceptible to criticism, not to mention the illusions placed in the 'tale of governance'.[232]

However, all hope is not lost.

Saad-Diniz[233] questions the need to develop alternative solutions to corporate responsibility as a possible preferred path 'for the prevention of economic

---

[225] Saad-Diniz (2019), p. 67.

[226] Saad-Diniz (2019), p. 70–71.

[227] Nieto Martín (2013b), p. 183.

[228] Nieto Martín (2013b), p. 178.

[229] Nieto Martín (2013b), p. 183.

[230] Nieto Martín (2019a), p. 146.

[231] In this sense: 'even though the practices of *compliance* and theoretical solutions are so adeptly incorporated as a "market product," it is believed there is much more than the commonplace prevention of economic infractions. Rather than a business obstacle, the technology of *compliance* can serve to secure a more privileged position in a less aggressive business environment, fairer and with clearer strategies to share the benefits of business with the community'. (Our translation). Saad-Diniz (2019), p. 20–21.

[232] Saad-Diniz (2015), p. 80.

[233] Saad-Diniz (2015), p. 80 ff.

infractions in the *game* of regulating *global businesses'*. Among the issues raised by the author, at this brief moment, and by way of conclusion, some complement the ideas presented so far.

Regarding corporate responsibility, in the last two decades, 'the Criminal Justice System has experienced the transition from strict liability to liability based on the structuring of organisational duties. More than that, the CJS has transformed traditional models of *business regulation enforcement'*.[234]

To address the insufficiency of realistic metrics on the effectiveness of responsive regulation and the consequent structural decoupling between regulators and the regulated, a more sophisticated approach to *compliance culture* is proposed through the provision of 'options of strategies and priorities that encourage participation at all levels of the public sphere and in relevant decision-making processes in the private environment',[235] as well as the creation, by self-regulation, of binding rules (*binding rules*) that are not formally or legally regulated, in order to mobilise, in a structural change, the distancing from negative solutions and the approach 'around positive solutions, aimed at exerting influence and effective impact on deviant corporate behaviour'.[236]

In another relevant aspect, Saad-Diniz points to the need to rethink the [excessive] application of [criminal] law beyond borders [extraterritoriality], appearing more prudent to 'respect corporate commitments, assist in protection or even affirm it more directly, address human rights from a more systematic and realistic dimension',[237] especially when considering the potential action of multinationals compared to states.[238]

Thus, an alternative solution is proposed to expand codes of conduct and integrity beyond borders, cultivating the effects of more effective ethical behaviour 'than "just" the traditional forms of law enforcement'.[239] Using new moral justifications in corporate decision-making processes, the criminal responsibility of the corporation would play a new role,[240] because 'ethical interpretations could be more incisive to reorganise infringing behaviours and reduce opportunities for corporate crime'.[241]

In this aspect, it is assumed that this corporate reorientation would align with new international *standards* of ethical behaviour dedicated 'to protecting the interests of stakeholders'[242] through accommodation in internal conduct structures, and the reservation of their interests related to the fraudulent or corrupt activity of

---

[234] Saad-Diniz (2015), p. 83.
[235] Saad-Diniz (2015), p. 84.
[236] Saad-Diniz (2015), p. 84.
[237] Saad-Diniz (2015), p. 86.
[238] Saad-Diniz (2015), p. 86.
[239] Saad-Diniz (2015), p. 86.
[240] Saad-Diniz (2015), p. 86.
[241] Saad-Diniz (2015), p. 86.
[242] Saad-Diniz (2015), p. 86.

the corporation. In the end, 'more than intimidating the *bad actors*, the idea is to encourage *doing the right thing*'.[243]

Another issue to be considered concerns the role of private regulation in corporate responsibility in relation to the process of ethical decision-making, that is, the role beyond corporate criminal liability, as well as the need to *take corporate criminal liability seriously*. It is pertinent to overcome the illusory obstacles of the *compliance culture*, to reflect on how business organisation structures affect the ethical decision-making processes of the individuals who make up the corporations, in order to requalify the debate for the transition from the threat of sanctions to the incentive to introduce ethics into global business.[244]

Thus, assuming that the use of criminal sanctions is an exceptional measure, the role of private regulation is highlighted to 'offer new regulatory standards and innovative alternatives to prevent corruption and protect human rights'.[245]

References

Books and Theses

Arroyo Zapatero, L., & Nieto Martín, A. (Eds.). (2013). *El derecho penal económico en la era compliance*. Valencia: Tirant lo Blanch.

Ayres, I., & Braithwaite, J. (1992). *Responsive regulation* (p. 101). Oxford University Press: New York.

Barrilari, C. (2018). *Crime empresarial, autorregulação e compliance*. São Paulo: Thomson Reuters

Brodowski, D. et al. (Eds.) (2014). *Regulating corporate criminal liability*. New York: Springer

OECD. (2011). *OECD guidelines for multinational enterprises*. Paris: OECD Publishing.

Rodrigues, A. M. (2019). *Direito penal económico: uma política criminal na era do compliance* (p. 45). Coimbra: Almedina.

Saad-Diniz, E. (2019). *Ética negocial e compliance: entre educação executiva e a interpretação judicial*. São Paulo: Thomson Reuters Brasil.

Sarcedo, L. (2014). *Compliance e responsabilidade penal da pessoa jurídica*: construção de um novo modelo de imputação, baseado na culpabilidade corporativa. Ph.D. Thesis, São Paulo: University of São Paulo

Shecaira, S. S. (2020). *Criminologia* (p. 502). 8th edn. São Paulo: Thomson Reuters.

Silveira, R. M. J. (2016). *Direito penal empresarial*: a omissão do empresário como crime. Belo Horizonte: D'Plácido.

Silveira, R. M. J., & Saad-Diniz, E. (2015). *Compliance, direito penal e lei anticorrupção* (p. 68). São Paulo: Saraiva.

Souza, A. B. G. (2021). *Direito penal empresarial: critérios de atribuição de responsabilidade e o papel do compliance*. São Paulo: LiberArs.

---

[243] Complementing this idea, the author continues, shortly thereafter: 'with the promotion of *doing the right thing* a new corporate culture can be introduced, not limited to moral subjectivism, but creating new spaces for a certain form of paternalistic thinking'. (Our translation). Saad-Diniz (2015), p.87.

[244] Saad-Diniz (2015), p. 88.

[245] Saad-Diniz (2015), p. 88.

Journal Articles

Braithwaite, J. (1982). Enforced self-regulation. *Michigan Law Review*, *80*(7), 1446–1507, 1470.
Braithwaite, J. (2000). The new regulatory state. *British Journal of Criminology*, *40*, 222–238.
Nieto Martín, A. (2007). ¿Americanización o europeización del Derecho Penal económico? *Revista Penal*, *19*, 120–135.
Nieto Martín, A. (2008). Responsabilidad social, gobierno corporativo y autorregulación: sus influencias en el derecho penal de la empresa. *Política Criminal*, *3*(5), 1–18
Nieto Martín, A. (2013a). La privatización de la lucha contra la corrupción. *Revista Penal México*, *4*, 133–143.
Nieto Martín, A. (2020). La autorregulación preventiva de la empresa como objeto de la política criminal. *EMERJ Journal*, *22*(2), 9–3
Nieto Martín, A. (2022). Compliance programs: una visión panorámica. *Revista Científica do CPJM*, *1*(3), 1–23.
Rodrigues, A. M. (2020). Crime econômico corporativo: governança e compliance como (novos) meios de socialização. *Revista Brasileira de Ciências Criminais*, *171*, 19–52, 40.
Saad-Diniz, E. (2018). Brasil versus Golias: os 30 anos da responsabilidade penal da pessoa jurídica e as novas tendências em compliance. *Revista dos Tribunais, São Paulo*, *107*(988), 25–53.
Silva Sánchez J-M (2008) La evolución ideológica de la discusión sobre la 'responsabilidad penal' de las personas jurídicas. Derecho Penal y Criminología *29*(86–87):129–148.
Souza, A. B. G. (2015). Programas de compliance e a atribuição de responsabilidade individual nos crimes empresariais. *Revista Portuguesa de Ciência Criminal*, *25*(1/4), 117–143, 124–125

Book Chapters

Barrilari, C. (2019). O cumprimento normativo. In A. Nieto Martín, E. Saad-Diniz, & R. G. Gomes (Eds.), *Manual de cumprimento normativo e responsabilidade das pessoas jurídicas* (2nd edn p. 57). São Paulo: Tirant Lo Blanch.
Lascuraín, J. A. (2018). La responsabilidad penal individual em los delitos de empresa. In N. J. Mata Barranco et al. (Eds.), *Derecho penal económico y de la empresa*. Madrid: Dykinson.
Laufer, W. (2014). Where is the moral indignation over corporate crime? In D. Brodowski et al. (Eds.), *Regulating corporate criminal liability* (p. 19–21). New York: Springer.
Laufer, W. S. (2015). O jogo do compliance. In E. Saad-Diniz et al. (Eds.), *Regulação do abuso no âmbito corporativo: o papel do direito penal na crise financeiras*. São Paulo: LiberArs.
Nieto Martín, A. (2013b). Problemas fundamentales del cumplimiento normativo en el derecho penal. In F. Llamacponcca Mendoza (coord) *Anuario de Derecho Penal. Núm. 2013–2014: Temas de derecho penal económico—empresa y compliance* (pp. 172–200). Salamanca: Editorial Fund.
Nieto Martín, A. (2019a). Compliance, criminologia e responsabilidade penal de pessoas jurídicas. In Nieto Martín A (Ed.), Saad-Diniz E, Gomes RG (Eds.), *Manual de cumprimento normativo e responsabilidade das pessoas jurídicas*, 2nd edn. Editora Tirant Lo Blanch, São Paulo.
Nieto Martín, A. (2019b). O cumprimento normativo. In A. Nieto Martín, E. Saad-Diniz, & R. G. Gomes (Eds.), *Manual de cumprimento normativo e responsabilidade das pessoas jurídicas*, 2nd edn. Editora Tirant Lo Blanch, São Paulo, pp. 29–61.
Nieto Martín A., & Moreno, B. (2019) A responsabilidade penal das pessoas jurídicas no direito comparado. In: Nieto Martín A (Ed.), Saad-Diniz E, Gomes RG (Eds.), Manual de

cumprimento normativo e responsabilidade das pessoas jurídicas, 2nd edn. Editora Tirant Lo Blanch, São Paulo.
Saad-Diniz, E. (2015). Regulação privada: há ainda alternativas para a prevenção à corrupção e proteção de direitos humanos no âmbito corporativo?. In E. Saad-Diniz, D. Brodowski, A. L. Sá (Eds.), *Regulação do abuso no âmbito corporativo*: *o papel do direito penal na crise financeira* (p. 82). São Paulo: LiberArs.
Saad-Diniz, E. (2015). Regulação privada: há ainda alternativas para a prevenção à corrupção e proteção de direitos humanos no âmbito corporativo?. In E. Saad-Diniz, D. Brodowski, & A. L. Sá (Eds.), *Regulação do abuso no âmbito corporativo*: *o papel do direito penal na crise financeira* (p. 8). São Paulo: LiberArs.
Sánchez, J. B. (2019). Corporate crime, human rights and human security. In N. Sans Mulas (Ed.), *Human rights 70 years after the universal declaration*. Tirant lo Blanch, Valencia.
Shecaira, S. S., & Sarcedo, L. (2014). A responsabilidade penal da pessoa jurídica. In J. C. Paschoal, & R. M. J Silveira (orgs) *Livro em homenagem a Miguel Reale Junior* (p. 690). Rio de Janeiro: G/Z.
Sieber, U. (2013). Programas de compliance no direito penal empresarial: um novo conceito para o controle da criminalidade. In W. T. Oliveira et al. (Eds.), *Direito Penal Econômico:* estudos em homenagem aos 75 anos do Professor Klaus Tiedemann (p. 291). São Paulo: LiberArs.

Legal Document

Brasil, Supremo Tribunal Federal (2013) Recurso Extraordinário 548.181. Relatora Min. Rosa Weber. 6 August 2013.

Online Sources

BBC News. (2018). The scandal that made Facebook lose US$35 billion. https://www.bbc.com/portuguese/internacional-43466255
Estadão. (2017). JBS shares fall 11%. https://economia.estadao.com.br/noticias/geral,acoes-da-jbs-e-da-brf-devem-ser-penalizadas-pela-operacao-carne-fraca,70001703746
International Organization for Standardization. (2025). ISO standards. https://www.iso.org/Moura
Moura, J. (2020). Carrefour shares fall more than 5%. *Folha de S. Paulo*, 23. November. https://www1.folha.uol.com.br/mercado/2020/11/acoes-do-carrefour-caem-mais-de-5-apos-assassinato-de-homem-negros.html
Moura, J. (2020). Carrefour shares fall more than 5% after murder of black man. Folha de S. Paulo, 23 Nov. 2020. https://www1.folha.uol.com.br/mercado/2020/11/acoes-do-carrefour-caem-mais-de-5-apos-assassinato-de-homem-negro.shtml. Accessed Apr 2025.

Chapter 5
Final Considerations

The work plan proposed to take as a contingent point of analysis by the criminal justice system, the harmful potential arising from corporate activity, notably those involved in the corruption scenario, considered in a broad spectrum.

In order to understand the current panorama surrounding the violation of human rights by corporations, an order of ideas was sought to integrate, as far as possible in methodological terms, the elements 'companies', 'human rights' and 'corruption'.

From now on, brief propositions will be articulated, and conclusions reached during this research.

Initially, the current scenario of human rights protection was presented, highlighting the fundamentality of its protection at an international level, especially considering, in the contemporary conception of human rights, the indispensability of cooperation between countries in safeguarding these rights in order to effectively reach a multi-level protection standard.

Highlighting the insufficiency of nation-states in remedying the problems faced in contemporary times—such as, in this analysis, the violation of human rights—it is guided by the need to formulate new contours to the Law, since, in crisis, it demands the combination of efforts to overcome its current scenario of 'void of guarantees' and 'fragility'.

In this 'new' law, guided by a network model, its postulation is converted into a set of integrations between various legal systems that emerges as the support of an interconstitutional, cooperative and solidary panorama among the States, with the assumption of new values such as creativity, flexibility, pluralism and reciprocal learning, in order to enable constructive links in the 'multicentric' society.

Therefore, in this scenario, the plausibility of adopting corporate self-regulation as a possible flexible legal element to engender formulations capable of achieving a cooperative relationship between legal orders, as well as promoting transversal and multidimensional relations in the multi-level protection of human rights, is evident. This is because, as an instrument derived from *soft law*, self-regulation presents itself as a component of permeability in the dialogic construction between jurisdictions.

L. d. B. Ibarra Papa, *Prevention of Human Rights Violations in the Corporate Sphere*, IBCCrim Studies in Criminal Law, Human Rights and Criminology 1,
https://doi.org/10.1007/978-3-032-06213-0_5

Indeed, the relevance of self-regulatory mechanisms is also highlighted in the emerging reality of corporations taking the lead in the international scenario, as they can, in some way, fill the *governance gap* existing in the transnational framework of corporate activities, especially because, due to the influence and economic power they exert, they position themselves as catalysts for addressing human rights violations, particularly in the *host states* where they are established.

It is within the scenario of the *human costs of corporate globalisation* that corporations are called upon to assume a role of responsibility in the protection of human rights. Thus, the international debate has been dedicated, in recent decades, to permeating the interface between 'business *and* human rights', notably with the diffusion of *soft law* instruments, such as the Guiding Principles on Business and Human Rights of 2011, as well as reflections on the fundamentality of adopting *hard law* to ensure greater coercibility or *enforcement* of the non-binding guidelines of *soft law*.

In this spectrum of corporate responsibilities in the face of human rights violations, the need to promote a combination of flexible norms and state *hard law* regulations is discussed, especially as a way to create a greater impact on the effectiveness of preventive instruments. In this field, the indispensability of articulated regulation, of *networked governance* or network governance, is mentioned, so that private regulatory mechanisms complement the traditional and formal role played by States in the protection of human rights.

Hence, the essentiality of the discussion about corporate self-regulation as a potential flexible legal source and part of a network legal model in promoting the prevention of violations of these rights. Further on, the possibility of corporate criminal liability playing the coercive role of *hard law* in counterbalance to *soft law* regulations is introduced into the debate.

Given this scenario pointed out in Chap. 2, the work inserts, in Chap. 3, the framework of combating corruption as a potential integrating element between mechanisms for preventing corporate crime and mitigating measures for human rights violations.

The combination of themes (companies, human rights and corruption), as seen, still lacks greater scientific cohesion—especially empirical data. However, the current legal reality of combating corruption emerges from the new panorama of imposing corporate standards of compliance and integrity—notably, in Brazil, from the Anti-Corruption Law.

When examining, specifically, corruption, it is noted that the possibility of joint efforts to prevent legal-penal goods and human rights arises from the self-constitution of companies and the integrity parameters currently in vogue, which, with clear influence from international instruments, are adopted by the Brazilian legal system.

Critiques have been raised regarding this internationalising trend of adopting (a priori) penal mechanisms of formal social control without prior reflections on potentially more efficient means to meet anti-corruption social demands. This often places the exercise of the *ius puniendi* at a level where it frequently acts to the detriment of the *ultima ratio* character of the penal system.

At this point, the debate on the legitimacy and the effects resulting from the choices of Brazilian criminal policy in controlling corruption through an excessively (and perhaps exclusively) repressive Penal Law proves pertinent. It emerges as necessary to have in perspective the current moment of corporate criminal law and the influences arising from contemporaneity, especially in order to ascertain to what extent the institutes of *criminal compliance* and the criminal liability of the legal person are justifiable.

Clearly, the examination of the current state of criminal policy in terms of corporate corruption has led to the analysis of criminal expansion and its imminent relationship with the aspirations of globalised risk society in the face of transnational delinquency. In this spectrum, the rise of the 'new' or 'modern' Penal Law is highlighted, adapting punitive structures to address this social 'call' for more pertinent (and potentially more severe) control measures.

In this new phase of Penal Science, the so-called Economic Penal Law is introduced, and the difficulties displayed in the protection of legal goods in the economic collective sphere are notably marked by the challenges in typifying the illicit and the frequent use of abstract danger crimes. Indeed, many of those criticisms regarding the excessive use of the penal branch are substantiated in these striking aspects, ultimately aimed at highlighting a possible legitimacy problem.

In the midst of the discussions, the need to seek political-criminal strategies that bring a balance between the excessive use of 'modern' criminal law and the impossibility of ignoring and confronting the increasingly relevant presence of corporate delinquency emerges. It is, therefore, notable that there is a need to implement more coherent responses that indicate a legitimate source of protection, adopting a 'penal prudence' with regard to the approach of criminal law in the economic field.

For this reason, in this context, self-regulation presents itself as a legitimate legal form to encompass a variation of the instruments of formal social control in the context of preventing corporate crime. This is, therefore, Penal Law in the era of *compliance*.

Thus, in order to understand this variation of Penal Law, oriented towards encouraging the formulation of corporate conduct codes as a source of crime prevention, the highlighted analysis of economic criminology is of great relevance, notably undertaking reflections on the criminal dynamics in corporate frameworks and assessing to what extent the contributions regarding *corporate crime* are capable of elucidating better prevention and restoration mechanisms.

In this way, criminological experience highlights not only the explanatory theories of criminal deviation in the corporate sphere but also underpins the necessary overcoming of current moral justifications imposed on the criminal justice system, guiding a more forceful direction of criminal policy towards corporate crime and the severe damages resulting from its implementation—for example, work, human rights violations.

Moreover, it was necessary to understand corporate victimisation processes as sources of more efficient criteria for reflections on the formulation of more sophisticated prevention instruments that take into account not only the search for dissuasive means of criminal practices but also direct attention to the restoration of damages caused by any crimes committed.

Thus, in the search for more effective and less 'cosmetic' *criminal compliance* instruments, the knowledge of corporate criminology reveals more forceful formulations in the construction of prevention methods and structures, especially those established from evidence and metrics filtered by it. In other words, these bases can inform, for example, about the possible margins or fields of criminal opportunity present in the corporation's activities, or even denote to what extent it is possible to verify the occurrence of the structural criminal type necessary to trigger the autonomous liability of the company.

Furthermore, it is possible to envisage that corporate victimology, combined with the mechanisms of participation of *stakeholders* in *compliance* programmes, can enhance the effectiveness of prevention, as it guides the interests involved beyond the activity developed by the company; that is, it allows social, human and environmental values of communities to be taken into account in the functioning of prevention techniques, as well as guiding lines in case the socially harmful corporate behaviour comes to violate them.

Finally, it was understood that the autonomous liability of the legal person (or mixed/hybrid model) could present itself as a viable strategy of criminal policy in order to scale the *law enforcement* of corporate regulatory compliance and ensure its greater yield.

In no other way, the criminological understanding regarding criminal activities within corporations is pointed out as a strategic element to extract better indicators about the defects of the organisation and also as a means to instrumentalise deterrent mechanisms directed at collective crime and assess to what extent it is possible to consider the inherent culpability of the legal entity for its socially harmful behaviours, such as the violation of human rights.

It is not unknown that these topics deserve greater precision and depth; thus, they stand out as points of pause, capable of continuation in the future: (i) the deeper understanding regarding the fruitful relationship between criminological contributions, organisational defect and the delimitation of the company's autonomous responsibility, as well as (ii) on victimological processes, the participation of *stakeholders* and the instrumentalisation of *compliance* programmes aimed at preventing the violation of human rights.

MIX
Papier aus verantwortungsvollen Quellen
Paper from responsible sources
FSC® C105338

If you have any concerns about our products,
you can contact us on
ProductSafety@springernature.com

In case Publisher is established outside the EU,
the EU authorized representative is:
Springer Nature Customer Service Center GmbH
Europaplatz 3, 69115 Heidelberg, Germany

Printed by Libri Plureos GmbH
in Hamburg, Germany